HAVE YOU MET THESE WOMEN?

BY

HAROLD JOHN OCKENGA

*Minister, Park Street Congregational Church
Boston, Mass.*

*Author of "These Religious Affections"
"Our Protestant Heritage"
"To Every One That Believeth"*

Second Edition

WIPF & STOCK · Eugene, Oregon

Wipf and Stock Publishers
199 W 8th Ave, Suite 3
Eugene, OR 97401

Have You Met These Women?
By Ockenga, Harold John and Rosell, Garth M.
Copyright©1940 by Ockenga, Harold John
ISBN 13: 978-1-5326-7415-0
Publication date 2/22/2019

DEDICATED TO THE WOMEN
OF PARK STREET CHURCH

SERIES FOREWORD
Harold John Ockenga: Voice of American Evangelicalism

HAROLD JOHN OCKENGA (1905–85) was one of the most remarkable individuals I have ever known. As a pastor and preacher, as a college president, as founder and president of two influential seminaries, as a popular writer of articles and books, as president of numerous organizations, and as one of the key leaders of the resurgent evangelical movement that swept across America and around the world during the mid-twentieth century, Ockenga's fame and influence were virtually unparalleled. "He was a giant among giants," reflected Billy Graham at Ockenga's funeral in 1985. "Nobody outside of my family influenced me more than he did. I never made a major decision without first calling and asking his advice and counsel. I thank God for his friendship and for his life."[1]

My own acquaintance with Ockenga came in 1978 when he invited me to join him as academic dean of the seminary where he was then serving as president. His passion for the spread of the Gospel around the world, his love for Christ and His church,

---

1. Billy Graham, "Harold John Ockenga: A Man Who Walked with God," *Christianity Today*, March 15, 1985, 35.

his deep commitment to spiritual renewal, his compelling vision for what theological education needed to become, and his unquestioned life of integrity persuaded me to accept his invitation. While working together at Gordon-Conwell Theological Seminary, Ockenga became my treasured mentor and friend. As we talked and prayed together, my appreciation for him deepened and my spiritual life was enriched.[2]

More than thirty years have passed since Harold John Ockenga walked among us.

Whole new generations have been born and have reached maturity with virtually no memory of this amazing leader and with only limited access to his most influential writings. The republication by Wipf and Stock Publishers of his major writings, including more than a dozen books and scores of articles, will now allow a new generation of readers to have access to the writings that helped shape an entire movement. Indeed, the book that you hold in your hands, like many of Ockenga's other publications, was eagerly read and put into action by the thousands of evangelical Christians who helped provide biblical guidance and fresh energy for mid-twentieth-century evangelicalism. With the appearance of this volume, by God's grace, it can once again provide guidance and fresh energy to a global movement in our own century—a movement that is increasingly in need of such godly guidance and wisdom.

Garth M. Rosell, Series Editor
Senior Research Professor of Church History
Gordon-Conwell Theological Seminary
South Hamilton, Massachusetts
January 1, 2017

2. Garth M. Rosell, *The Surprising Work of God: Harold John Ockenga, Billy Graham, and the Rebirth of Evangelicalism* (Grand Rapids: Baker Academic, 2008) 11–38.

FOREWORD

Woman! Creature of caprice. God's noblest and last handiwork. Source of inspiration and degradation. Goddess, temptress, power over man, plaything of man, turning point of character, instrument of fate, ruler of history, ennobling, debasing, full of virtue, capable of basest crime, loving, hating, tender, violent, strange paradox of life.

Do you know woman? God draws the picture of every kind of woman. Good women, to whom man owes his greatest debts—his mother, his sister, his wife, his sweetheart. Evil women, to whom man must give a wide berth, so as to escape their schemes and influence. A woman may lead man to heaven or to hell. God tells of their kinds and their characteristics, in the Bible.

These ten sermons are selected from a much longer series preached on Sunday evenings in the Park Street Church, Boston. They are printed under the same titles and in the same form as when delivered. The identity of these women was not revealed until each sermon was preached, and for the purpose of stimulating curiosity in the women of the Bible, they were not presented in normal Biblical order. Keen interest in Bible study was sustained through the entire series.

TABLE OF CONTENTS

I.	THE WOMAN WHO RUINED A HOLY MAN	9
II.	THE WOMAN WHO COMMANDED A MAN'S LOVE	22
III.	THE WOMAN WHO LAUGHED AT GOD	36
IV.	THE WOMAN WHO WON A HUSBAND	49
V.	THE WOMAN WHOSE SON WAS GREATEST OF MEN	64
VI.	THE WOMAN WHO TURNED TEMPTRESS	79
VII.	THE WOMAN WHO WAS BETRAYED	93
VIII.	THE WOMAN WHO MADE A HOUSE A HOME	107
IX.	THE WOMAN WHO COULD NOT FORGET	121
X.	THE NOBLEST WOMAN OF ALL	135

I

THE WOMAN WHO RUINED A HOLY MAN

She made him sleep upon her knees; and she called for a man, and she caused him to shave off the seven locks of his head; and she began to afflict him, and his strength went from him.

THE cavalcade of women whom we cause to pass before your eyes begins with one of the most infamous women of the Old Testament—a wicked woman who takes her place alongside of Judas as base, false, and evil. We would rather begin with wickedness and end with righteousness in order to show what redemption does to human nature. Just as there are more good than evil women recorded in the Bible and as there are more good than evil women in life, so there will be in this series of sermons.

There were many good women in the ancestry of Christ, but when the Holy Spirit singled out four of them to be included in His genealogy, whom did He choose? Sarah, Rachel, and the godly women? No. He chose Tamar, notorious for shameful fornication; Rahab, given to the abomination of harlotry; Ruth, a despised Moabitess, who was forbidden access to the congregation; and Bathsheba, with whom David sinned. Herein we have illustrations of how the Lord saves through faith, delivers from natural punishment, and secures our salvation. We wish to emphasize this same redemptive process in singling out women of the Bible for study.

In the first instance, we choose Delilah, *The Woman Who Ruined a Holy Man.* Let us look, first, at the man who was ruined, namely, Samson; second, at the woman who ruined him, namely, Delilah; and third, at the ruin which engulfed them both.

I. THE MAN WHO WAS RUINED, NAMELY, SAMSON

We have called Samson the man who was ruined. His life impresses us as one gigantic ruin. That it once was beautiful and effective for God there can be no doubt, for the Book of Hebrews enrolls him as one of the heroes of the faith, of whom the world was not worthy. In him God had built a structure that was magnificent, but Samson himself brought it to ruin through the influence of a woman.

That Samson merits the title of a holy man is evident from the statements about his life. As with Isaac, Samuel, and John the Baptist, a supernatural element is connected with him in his birth. The angel of the Lord appeared unto the aged wife of Manoah with the promise, "Thou shalt conceive and bear a son." Later the annunciation was made unto Manoah. This child was to be a supernatural gift of God unto these righteous parents. The angel even went into detail as to the prenatal influences that would be brought to bear upon the son. The mother was to drink no wine nor strong drink and was to be exceedingly careful concerning unclean things mentioned in the Jewish Law.

It is significant that when God wants a man, He usually begins to prepare that man through his parents. If our own day is to produce leaders who are able to preserve our American heritage, it will be necessary for God to begin with the mothers and find some who will be separated unto His will before ever the children are born.

Manoah performed a sacrifice unto the angel and we read that the angel "did wondrously." He ascended into the sky in the presence of Manoah and his wife, and Manoah said, "We have seen the Lord." Undoubtedly this was none other than He whose name is called "Wonderful." In due time the child was born, and they named him "Samson," or "Sunny," because of the light hair, ruddy complexion, and bright disposition of the boy. He was a joy to the hearts of his father and mother, who had longed for such a possession.

The Woman Who Ruined a Holy Man

The angel had said, "The child shall be a Nazarite unto God from the womb." To take the vow of a Nazarite meant to separate oneself unto the Lord. The sign of this was that the individual partook of no wine or strong drink whatsoever; that he let his hair grow in seven locks, which were braided back of his head; and that he observed the laws concerning the defilement of the body. Note that when one was to be sanctified and separated unto the Lord he was to touch no liquor. The great generals of history, such as Caesar, Charlemagne, Gustavus Adolphus, Frederick the Great, Cromwell, and Napoleon, with the single exception of Alexander the Great, were men given to temperance. They knew that liquor and a clear head do not go together. If a man would be holy unto the Lord he must abstain from all use of liquor. Not only was the Nazarite, Samson, to abstain, but also his parents were commanded to abstain. The only adequate principle toward liquor is total abstinence. John the Baptist was also a Nazarite, and the clearer picture of him in the common mind might help to clarify the indistinct picture of Samson. It was the custom of men such as Paul to take upon them a Nazarite vow for a particular length of time, but the Baptist and Samson were Nazarites from birth. The vow was a symbol of the consecration of an individual unto the Lord.

During Samson's youth, he was possessed of mighty strength and physical power. If the craven, degenerated, almost despicable Israelites of Samson's day had only seen what it would have meant to have been visited by the Spirit of the Lord and what God could have done with a nation so consecrated unto Him, they would not have been vassals of the Philistines and the Canaanites. Samson's strength was simply an evidence of a supernatural power given to him by God. Hence, during his youth, he made intermittent forays into the Philistines' country, playing huge jokes upon them and usually delivering himself by his cleverness and his great strength.

As a young man, it was evident that Samson was established to be a judge in Israel. He was a great deliverer, and he judged the nation for twenty years. Our knowledge of the conditions of the people are drawn from the Book of Judges, where it says, "Every man did that which was right in his own eyes." There, sodomy among the Benjamites caused the rest of the Israelites to wipe out the entire tribe with the exception of six hundred people. There, as craven slaves of the Philistines for nearly a hundred years, the Israelites went down to the country of the Philistines to sharpen their instruments of agriculture. No swords were allowed in that nation. There the priests committed adultery with the women of the land. In the midst of these sons of Belial, Samson attempted to judge the nation on the basis of God's law. However, the promise made unto Manoah was that Samson should begin to deliver Israel. There is an implication here that he would not complete the deliverance, and he certainly did not. Under the Spirit of God, Samson constituted the only bulwark against the Philistines, who at that period had reached the height of their material prosperity and military strength. The degeneration of his own countrymen was shown when a thousand of them bound him on one occasion and turned him over to the Philistines instead of assisting him to deliver the country from the dominion of the Philistines. During those twenty years as judge of Israel, Samson was striving to do what was right. He was a symbol of self-control and of consecration. Though the sons of Belial waited for his halting, he alone walked with God in a position of power and holiness.

Samson's power was dependent entirely upon his obedience and his separation. The Lord had chosen Samson for a purpose. He had made a covenant with him before his birth, the sign of which was the Nazarite vow. The parents of Samson were righteous and godly people and not only rehearsed to him the conditions that were revealed to

The Woman Who Ruined a Holy Man 13

them before his birth, but they explained to him the meaning of the Nazarite vow and the need of Israel for a great deliverer in their day. Their hopes for this child were high, and they taught him to know the Lord and to observe his part of the conditions imposed by God's covenant.

At least the Spirit of God was upon him and enabled him to do great exploits. Samson was an example of the text, "they that know their God shall be strong and do exploits." On one occasion he rent a lion as he would a kid. He alone composed an army able to defeat a thousand Philistines. He could lift up the gates of a city and carry them bodily up to the top of a hill and deposit them in scorn of the enemy. Samson was a man of riddles, and one who jested with the enemy and who presumed on his own strength. Samson had to learn that it is not by might nor by power but by the Spirit of the Lord.

Though there were many and wonderful things in the life of Samson, none of them are recorded for us, not even a single case that he judged in Israel, yet the story of his temptation and his weakness and his fall are presented to us in vivid language in order that they may be a warning to us. The point of Samson's weakness was women. Like Solomon, he loved many strange women, and they became a snare unto him.

First, there was the case of the daughter of Timnath. On one of his expeditions into the country of the Philistines he saw a beautiful face and was lured by it. Quite often love leaps the boundaries of race, creed, and country, leading men into strange unions. Much to the consternation of his parents, on his return he asked that they get that woman for him. His parents remonstrated, saying, "Is there never a woman among the daughters of thy brethren that thou goest to take a wife of the uncircumcised Philistines?" But Samson could only answer, "Get her for me, for she pleases me well." Sadness and sorrow descended upon his parents because they saw that this was the beginning of trouble for their wonderful son. The story is a sad experience. It involved days of weeping for Samson's wife, days of disappointment for him, and ultimately death for the entire family of the unfortunate girl who was involved in this episode.

The next woman with whom Samson was involved was another Philistine in the capital of their country, Gaza. She was a common sinner of the city, and Samson became enamored with her. We can make no excuse for a man of God being guilty of an action like this, and the Scripture makes no excuse for him either. Samson had again succumbed to his own weakness. It is true that in the midst of the night his conscience warned him and he rose up in time to save his life, delivering himself by a mighty exploit of strength, but his downward path had begun. One cannot take fire into his bosom and not be burned. God had mercy upon Samson at this time, but it was of no avail.

The third woman with whom Samson became involved was Delilah, another daughter of the Philistines, who had her home in the beautiful Valley of Sorek. In those days, Palestine's hills were covered with trees, and her valleys had streams of water, and thousands of people inhabited the land. Timnath and Sorek and Gaza were all near together in the south country of the Philistines. Here, beside a quiet river, Delilah had a garden and a home where she entertained her callers. Broken homes are due to women such as this. Our cities in America are full of them. It is because of them that divorces occur in one out of every five marriages. One wonders what a man expects to have when he exchanges a wife and a home for a woman such as this. A careful look at Samson ought to be a strong warning to any who are beset by such a sin. Samson's fall had begun with lust. First, the lust of the eyes, and then the lust of the flesh. Then he proceeded to lying, and finally to abandoning his Nazarite vow and his contact with God. Samson had had ample warning against taking up

with another Philistine woman after his experiences with
the daughter of Timnath and with the woman of Gaza, and
the fact that he went on is not only a reproach upon a judge
of Israel but is a sad commentary upon the weakness of
the man. Thus we behold him as one placed in a high
position, elevated to the pinnacle of glory for those times,
and yet destined to a most disgraceful fall because he sinned
against the Spirit of God.

II. THE WOMAN WHO RUINED HIM, NAMELY, DELILAH

Anyone passing along the Valley of Sorek toward Eshtaol would have seen this beautiful little home with its vineyard and olive trees supported by the money of illicit love. It was inhabited by a famous but beautiful woman named Delilah. Probably this was not her true name but one assumed for her profession. Some think that Samson was married to this woman, but the Scripture gives no implication of this. She was merely the woman of Samson's choice in the hour of his weakness. The woman a man chooses reveals what he is. Delilah was physically beautiful but wanton. She misused her feminine appeal to an unusually disgraceful extent, but every woman who feigns love and indulges vanity and coquetry in order to obtain selfish ends is essentially like Delilah. Feminine charm is the gift of God. A woman has received it from her Creator. The appeal of love is that within the power of a woman, and God will certainly hold woman responsible for trifling with and misusing this fairest and best gift.

Delilah was brilliant and entertaining. Few men are infatuated over a long period of time only with beauty. One can hardly think that the fifty-year-old Julius Caesar would have become enamored and held over a long period of time by the twenty-one-year-old Cleopatra had she not been of a brilliant and entertaining nature as well as beautiful. Samson was irresistibly drawn to Delilah and returned to visit her often because she dazzled him with her wit and her brilliance. Delilah was unbelieving and hence was representative of heathen women. Heathenism knew nothing of the home life that Christianity has created. Woman was either a slave or she was a plaything of man. She was never considered his equal and never entered into the public life of a man. For their banquets and their public affairs, the heathen of antiquity depended upon a class of women such as Delilah. That Samson should have known better is very evident, but so should thousands of other men and women who even marry outside of their own religion. You simply cannot mix Christianity and unbelief, but it is impossible to tell young people this. They invariably come back in tears and heartache and disappointment because of the misunderstandings and the sorrows that arise therefrom. The Scripture says, "Be not unequally yoked together with unbelievers. What concord hath Christ with Belial?" It is no better to marry outside of the Christian faith today than it was to marry an unbeliever in the days of Samson. The person Samson chose was anything but a helpmate for a holy man of God.

From the narrative, we may quickly sketch the character of Delilah. First, she was selfish. It is clear from her dealings with the Philistines that she was covetous of money and wealth. She was ambitious, and she used Samson only to gain materially. Being proud of her ability as a lovemaker, she gloried in the fact that she was able to conquer the affections of the great Israelitish judge.

Second, she was false to the core. One might argue that she acted in behalf of her own country in order to deliver it from a great enemy and was only like unto Jael, who delivered the Israelites from Sisera, but the difference is that Jael never sold her husband or her lover for a price. Among women, Delilah takes her place as Judas does among men as a great traitor who sold a friend for a bribe.

Third, Delilah used her love for ulterior purposes. From the love Samson carried for her she could have responded

The Woman Who Ruined a Holy Man

and been true, but she only feigned love. In Delilah we have a woman with no principle, who was evil in every way in which we approach her character.

The influence of Delilah over Samson was stronger the more repeated the contacts became between the two. Samson's fall and ruin began in his first visit. The Scripture says, "There is a way which seemeth right unto a man, but the end thereof is death." Samson beheld these same practices on every hand round about him, yet he succumbed and became enslaved by this witch. He exchanged the glories of being judge of Israel and a servant of God, a Nazarite, for being the temporarily satisfied companion of a wanton woman. The influence of Delilah was entirely evil. It is true that a woman may lead a man either to heaven or to hell.

Delilah became the instrument of the Philistine lords. They, too, knew the weakness of Samson's nature, and so they offered her eleven hundred pieces of silver if she would deliver him into their hands. Delilah consented, and the result was a struggle of wit and love. One day Delilah said, "Tell me where your great strength lieth, Samson, and why it is that no one can bind you in order to overcome you at any time? You have done such wonderful things. What is the secret of it all?"

This should have revealed to Samson the desire of Delilah but, being so infatuated, he could not see through her craft. Jokingly, he replied that if they would bind him with seven green withes that were never dried, then he should be weak as any other man. While Samson slept, she so bound him and informed the Philistines to wait outside her chamber. Then she cried, "The Philistines be upon thee, Samson," and he rose up and broke the bonds as if they were a thread touched by the fire. He had mocked her, and inwardly she was very impatient and angry, but subtly she only reproached him for his lack of love, finally protesting that if he really loved her he ought not to keep any secrets from his dear Delilah,

After her third failure, she said, "How canst thou say, 'I love thee' when thine heart is not with me? Thou hast mocked me these three times and hast not told me wherein thy great strength lies." It must have seemed to him that his sin became less sinful in that he had given himself to a woman who in spite of her illicit practices had such an ideally beautiful conception of love. She pressed him day by day, and his soul was vexed unto death until he told her all his heart, namely, that the source of his strength was his Nazarite vow, that if his hair were shaved from him he would be as weak as any other man. This time Delilah saw that he had told her all his heart, so she summoned the Philistines and had them ready for the final assault. Samson should have been warned as to the nature of a Philistine woman by the seven days' weeping of the daughter of Timnath, which won from him his former secret of the riddle, but instead he allowed himself to be deceived and by a self-revelation of the secret of his power he broke his compact with God. She had attained her purpose.

III. The Ruin That Finally Engulfed Samson

Delilah caused Samson to sleep across her lap, and she called for a Philistine to come and shave off his hair. How the man must have trembled as he performed his task delicately and gently so as not to awake the giant! Once finished, she cried, "Samson, the Philistines be upon thee." He awoke out of his sleep and said as at other times, "I will go out and shake myself," and he wist not that the Spirit of the Lord had departed from him. This is one of the saddest verses in the Bible. It depicts the state of a man who has known God and who has lost Him. It is the tragic state of being shelved in God's service. Concerning this, Paul said, "I keep under my body, and bring it into subjection; lest that by any means, when I have preached to others, I myself should be a castaway." What he meant was that God should shelve him in his effective service. It is tragic, once having known the Spirit of the Lord, to have grieved Him away. Paul wrote, "Grieve not the Spirit of God whereby we are sealed against the day of redemption." Any besetting sin, any disobedience, any wickedness or evil in the life of the believer, may cause him to grieve the Spirit of the Lord and thus to lose the victory.

Samson had been the great strong man, the unconquerable one, the overcomer, but once he had grieved the Spirit of the Lord away, he lost his victory. Without the Spirit of the Lord, the source of his strength, his power, his victory, and his exploits was gone. It was not Samson's hair that was the source of his strength: it was the fact that the hair was the symbol of the covenant between him and God, and when he broke the covenant by sin, God removed the Spirit of victory and power. It is all too common to see some spiritual giant of God, who has for ten, twenty, or forty years preached the gospel of Christ with tremendous power and victory, ultimately stripped of the source of his power. On numerous occasions we have listened to men who have boasted of their past deeds but who today are doing absolutely nothing for their Lord. This is a tragic situation.

Samson went out and shook himself and thought he would defend himself from the Philistines, but he found that his strength had gone and they were able to afflict him and conquer him. Delilah had done what a battalion of Philistine soldiers had failed to do. How she must have gloried in the power of her attraction and in the fame she received therefrom! Samson's was a rude awakening. He did not know that the Spirit of God had departed from him. What an awakening comes to a person, a child of God, who through sin has lost the blessing of the Lord and as a result finds that he can no longer overcome the innumerable difficulties that beset him round about. The Philistines expressed their hatred and spite on him in gouging out his eyes, in binding him, and in afflicting him. They had discerned his weakness, and they had defeated him by it. Be sure that Satan knows exactly where your besetting sin lies and where your weakest point is, and he will strike you there again and again through temptation until you either defeat him once and for all or he brings you low.

The next scene in Samson's life is in the prison in Gaza. This prison is in the bottom of the house of Dagon, a god of the Philistines. There, in deep humiliation, Samson labors as a slave along with the other slaves, grinding at the mill. He is bound in fetters of brass and has only enough liberty to perform his task. Visitors pass by and laugh, jeer, and call out upon him asking, "Where is your strength now? Where is the God of Israel? Why do you not do some exploit now?" Samson's only reply is to grind more fiercely. There is a legend that Milton has incorporated in his great poem called "Samson Agonistes," in which Delilah is supposed to have come to visit Samson in his prison-house in order to implore his forgiveness for her base deed. He cries out:

> *Out! Out! hyena, these are thy wonted arts,*
> *And arts of every woman false like thee;*
> *To break all faith, all vows, deceive, betray.*
> *Then as repentant, to submit, beseech,*
> *And reconcilement move with feign'd remorse.*

Then Delilah urges her weakness, saying: "Nor shouldst thou have trusted that to woman's frailty." Then she adds, "Ere I to thee, thou to thyself was cruel." To which Samson replies, "How cunningly the sorceress displays her own transgressions to upbraid me mine!"

Delilah's statement was true. Before any woman can betray him or be cruel to him, man must betray and be cruel to himself. Yet Samson now made a final renunciation of her and turned his heart back to God. We know this because it says, "The hair of his head began to grow again after he was shaven." The entire implication is that Samson in the

The Woman Who Ruined a Holy Man 21

prison-house remembered the heights from which he fell, remembered his fellowship with God, and remembered that the source of his power and strength was in the Lord, and so turned unto Him.

The story ends with a bright spot in the life of Samson. He had grievously sinned, and that sin had laid him low. His besetting sin had found him out, and he was defeated by it. As he was in the depths, during a great assembly of the Philistines, he was brought out to make sport, and before them he danced, broke beams, and demonstrated what strength he had, until weary. He asked the lad who led him to take him to the pillars of the house that he might rest. In that vast chamber there were some three thousand Philistines mocking him and praising their god for delivering him into their hands. Then Samson called upon the Lord and said, "O Lord God, remember me, I pray Thee, and strengthen me, I pray Thee, only this once, O God, that I may be at once avenged of the Philistines for my two eyes." Here he recognized that God was the source of his strength and of his blessing, and he turned unto Him. Samson had lost the presence of God, but he was not himself lost. His punishment was temporal, but the eternal guilt of his sin was remitted. A final gift of strength was given to him in answer to his prayer. He bowed himself, pulled on the pillars, and died in the mighty crash that followed. Here stands a man in whose life sin abounded, but grace did much more abound. By one act of repentance, he returned unto the Lord and was forgiven. So may you.

II

THE WOMAN WHO COMMANDED A MAN'S LOVE

> *And Jacob served seven years for Rachel and they seemed unto him but a few days, for the love he had to her.*

WE have selected the title, "A Woman Who Commanded a Man's Love," for Rachel. We use the word "command" in the sense in which it is used when we say of a woman, "She commands my respect," or "She commands my admiration," or "She commands my loyalty." It was in this sense that Rachel commanded the love of Jacob. Moreover, we have used the word "love" in its highest sense.

There is no other case recorded in the Bible of such abiding love as that which Jacob had for Rachel. This, in fact, is the best type of Christ's love for the church that is given to us. He loved her from the very beginning; he suffered for her; and he loved her to the end in spite of the blemishes in her character.

There is another love recorded in secular history somewhat similar to the love of Jacob for Rachel, which stimulated the man who possessed it to a marvelous achievement. I speak of Dante's love for Beatrice Portinari. This love inspired his life and enlarged his soul to the extent that he devoted his genius to her eulogy. Dante was born in the year 1265 and met Beatrice when he was only nine years old, but he at once conceived the highest and most enduring love for her. During the next nine years he met her only on one other occasion, during which she bestowed on him a celestial smile of recognition. Three years later, at the age of twenty-four, she died, and Dante determined to

The Woman Who Commanded a Man's Love 23

write of her such as was never written of any woman. Dante was a member of what is called the Guelf Party, composed of the common people in Florence and allied with Roman Catholicism. The opposing party was called the Ghebelline Party and was composed of the imperial, or state, unit. During Dante's life there was a constant struggle between the two, and while he was absent from Florence at one time his enemies secured his banishment. Thereafter he wandered throughout the cities of Italy engaged in literary work until he died at the age of fifty-six at Ravenna. Dante had married a daughter of one of the leaders of the Guelf Party and was the father of eight children but never during his life did he lose his idealistic love for Beatrice. Hence it was to her that he raised the monument of his love. No writer since the rise of the Romantic Schools of literature, when love became the chief theme of poetry, has so reverently worshiped and so happily embodied the highest ideals of womanhood as Dante. Here love was unrequited and in sorrow, anguish, and tears its possessor was driven to despair. It was the image of this gentle vision that warmed and purified his soul, and inspired his deeds until he became the "voice of ten silent centuries." She became a comforting, guiding spirit and illumined with intense joy the poet's heart, hitherto one of the saddest in all Christendom.

Thus it was that Dante—hereafter to be known to the world as the noblest of all lovers, when Dante the statesman, the philosopher, the Guelphic leader shall be forgotten—vowed that "if it would please Him by whom all things live, he would say of her that which had never been said of any lady." She became his muse. It was a message from her which led him down through the gates of Despair, across the Limbo that trembled with the sighs of hopeless longing, past Minos, judge of Hades, into the flaming City of Dis, garrisoned and guarded by demons and furies, past the Hell of Violence, where murderers and tyrants are forever steeped in the boiling blood waves of the Plegethon; through the increasing horrors of Circles, Evil-pits, and Bealts of Treachery; then up the toilsome steps of Purgatory, until at last appeared, drawn in the bosom of a cloud of flowers, thrown by angel hands, the radiant form of Beatrice clad in white, green, and red emblems of faith, hope, and charity. Thus this love for a young woman whom he had seen only twice in his life caused Dante to be remembered throughout the ages.

Likewise, the one ennobling influence in the life of Jacob was his love for Rachel. Through Rachel, God brought retribution to Jacob for his many sins in order to purify his soul. The beginning of this was the deception wrought on Jacob by Laban, the father of Rachel, when, after Jacob had served seven years for her, he was given the veiled Leah in the night and learned that he must serve a second seven years for the object of his love. There Jacob must have seen the hand of God requiting him for the deception he had wrought over the eyes of his old father in taking Esau's blessing. The next time his love for Rachel led him to recognize the hand of God was when he was returning from Padanaram and met a messenger who said that Esau was coming to meet him with four hundred armed men. Jacob knew that his own life and the life of his entire company were hanging by a thread. The prayer he prayed unto God by Peniel before he wrestled with the angel reveals to us what was uppermost in Jacob's mind. He said, "Deliver me, I pray Thee from the hand of Esau: for I fear him, lest he will come and smite me, and the mother with the children." It was the thought of Rachel and Rachel's child Joseph and the one who was yet to be born that drove Jacob to his knees as he wrestled with the angel of God. Finally, the Lord dealt with Jacob through the death of Rachel and the loss of her children, both Joseph and Benjamin, one of whom was sold into Egypt and the other of whom was compelled to go thence because of the

The Woman Who Commanded a Man's Love

famine, so that Jacob said to his other sons, "My son shall not go down with you for his brother is dead and he is left alone. If mischief befall him by the way in which he goes, then shall ye bring down my gray hairs with sorrow to the grave." The loss of Benjamin, the last of his family by Rachel, would have been the final straw in Jacob's sorrow. Thus we see that by his great love which Jacob bore to Rachel, God chastened and purified his soul. Woman has been the divine instrument in the salvation of man in all ages; for the love he bears her he is lifted to nobility, to purity, and to sacrificial living. A woman who can command his love can command the best of which he is capable.

I. The Incidents That Led to Their Meeting

Providence has a place in the bringing of two streams of life together. This must be recognized not only with Jacob and Rachel but in the uniting of any young man and young woman in love. Marriage was instituted of God so that one life may supplement another. Rebecca was exactly the opposite of Isaac, but her dynamic nature was just what passive Isaac needed. Just so, Rachel took her position in relation to Jacob. He needed a mooring for his emotions. He needed an anchor for his wandering soul, and he found that abiding place in Rachel. Never do I stand before a couple presenting themselves for marriage without thinking of the long line of history each represents and how now they will be merged as two great rivers are merged, thus strengthening one another and empowering one another. They come together to purify and to bless. Thus it was meant to be. Moreover, we always think of the ordering of events so that these two streams of life should come together and thus remember that Providence had a hand in it. Sometimes observers of a wedding or of a romance cannot see what a man sees in the woman or the woman sees in the man, but there is a purpose in it. The parents of Samson could not understand why he passed by all the beautiful daughters of the Israelites and became enamored with the Philistine woman who dwelt at Timnath and asked for her for his wife, but the Scripture says that God sought an occasion against the Philistines. The purpose was that Samson through this incident should be established as judge over the Israelites, whom he thereafter ruled for twenty years. Many were the previous events that prepared Jacob for his mother's weariness with the women whom his brother Esau had married and which were emblematic of his apostasy and his disobedience. Every married person may trace the events that led to his union with another person. Sometimes it is a chance meeting in a library or on a street-car or in a church or at a party, an incident that happened only because some other less important incident occurred before, and the whole course of life was changed. Thus we affirm that Providence has a part in bringing people together in marriage.

A second thing that contributed to Jacob's going to Haran was his early waywardness. This had its roots in his mother's partiality. From the beginning it seemed that Rebecca favored Jacob, whereas Isaac loved Esau, and there was a house divided against itself. Why was Rebecca so partial to Jacob? We know that Isaac loved Esau because he ate of his son's venison. Perhaps Rebecca's prejudice was due to the promise the Lord made to her before the birth of her son, which said, "The elder shall serve the younger." Paul later quotes this promise, saying, "That the purpose of God according to election might stand." From the divine side, Jacob was elected, but from the human side Rebecca pushed him by partiality. Undoubtedly this mother taught her son the value of the family succession and of the paternal inheritance because of the Messianic promise that had been made to Eve and had been reiterated to Sarah. About these things Esau did not care. At an early age, Jacob recognized their value

The Woman Who Commanded a Man's Love

and learned that life had a purpose. Hence it was inevitable that family rivalry between the one who inherited the blessing and did not value it and the one who did not inherit it but did value it, should ensue. We all know the story of Jacob's purchase of Esau's birthright for a mess of pottage. Esau had already revealed his tendency to apostasy in the women he had married, and now he despised his birthright. The New Testament says in warning to professors of Christianity, "Lest there be any fornicator or profane person such as Esau who for one morsel of meat sold his birthright. For ye know how that afterward when he would have inherited the blessing, he was rejected for he found no place of repentance though he sought it carefully with tears." Jacob was exceedingly clever in the timing of his offer and in appealing to Esau's weakest point, but nevertheless it was a transaction by which the younger son acquired the right to the patriarchal blessing that belonged to the elder son. The Scripture places the responsibility upon Esau, for he treated it as of no moment and of no value. Later, when Isaac was growing old Esau sought to obtain the blessing, because he then understood its value, but that did not invalidate the contract into which he had entered with Jacob. Hence Jacob again stooped to get what he thought was now his own and by deception he received the patriarchal blessing. Both men were wrong. God had said that Jacob was chosen, but how God would have brought it about in His own good time we are not told. Even though Jacob deserved the blessing, we make no excuse for his use of deception in receiving it. Then with bitter cries and tears, Esau sought it with repentance but to no avail.

The smouldering quarrel now broke out into the open and became too strong to keep both sons in one household. Esau plotted to murder Jacob, which is another mark of the type of character found in Esau. The word of his plan came to Rebecca's ears, so she determined to save Jacob and also at the same time to get him a wife of the kind God required. She decided to send him to her kinspeople in Haran until Esau's anger had cooled. Her punishment in participating in the deception of the aged and weak Isaac consisted in her never seeing her beloved and favorite son again. He departed for a twenty year sojourn, and ere he returned she had died. The Scripture implies that Jacob's departure was sudden, without taking leave of Esau. Isaac's agreement was gained to it by Rebecca, and without any personal attendants, and with little preparation, Jacob departed. What loneliness, fear, and discouragement beset his pathway by the time he had made one day's journey and rested at Bethel is revealed in that old hymn, which tells the story:

Though like the wanderer,
The sun gone down,
Darkness be over me,
My rest a stone;
Yet in my dreams I'd be
Nearer, my God, to Thee,
Nearer to Thee.

There let the way appear,
Steps unto heaven;
All that Thou sendest me
In mercy given;
Angels to beckon me
Nearer, my God, to Thee,
Nearer to Thee.

Then, with my waking thoughts,
Bright with Thy praise,
Out of my stony griefs,
Bethel I'll raise;
So by my woes to be
Nearer, my God, to Thee,
Nearer to Thee.

II. THE STORY OF THEIR IDYLLIC LOVE

Jacob and Rachel met at the old well in Haran. In the Near Eastern countries, courtship does not take place as it does here in the west. Here we want to be alone to speak our words in secret. There courtship is made in the open and usually at the well. Thus it was that Moses won his wife by a well in Midian. Jacob had completed his long journey by foot from Canaan and now was ready to rest by the well of Haran. As he approached it, he saw three flocks waiting to be watered. He greeted two of the men who were the shepherds of two flocks, saying, "Know ye Laban the son of Nahor?" and they replied, "We know him." Jacob asked, "Is he well?" They replied, "He is well and behold Rachel his daughter cometh with the sheep." As yet Jacob could not see Rachel distinctly, so he told them to water their sheep, and they replied, "We cannot until all the flocks be gathered together, until they roll the stone from the well's mouth," and thus it was evident that a huge slab of rock was used to keep the well from all defilement.

By this time, Rachel arrived with her father's sheep, for she was a shepherdess. Then are written these important words, "When Jacob saw Rachel." When he saw her, it was love at first sight. Jacob simply fell all over himself to please her. Empowered by such a desire, he performed a feat of great strength in rolling the stone away from the well. Then he watered Rachel's entire flock as an act of gallantry while these strangers looked on. Finally, he picked her up and kissed her. The Scripture adds, "And he wept." Rachel must have reminded him of his mother, of home and all that he had left behind, and the lonely man wept for joy to find a relative of his mother and especially a woman such as Rachel.

This love of Jacob, which was born at the well, never changed through his long life. Some men are gallant and loving before marriage but soon forget it afterward. It was not so with Jacob. His love increased with the passing days and years. Jacob never had an eye for anyone else than for Rachel. Undoubtedly Rachel changed in appearance in the hard experiences of her primitive life, and she did not always look as fresh and appealing as she did that day by the well, but Rachel always remained the light of Jacob's eyes. When as an old man in Egypt, Jacob came to his last sickness and was speaking his final words to Joseph, he referred to Rachel, saying, "As for me, when I came from Padan, Rachel died by me in the land of Canaan in the way, when yet there was but a little way to come to Ephrath, and I buried her there in the way of Bethlehem." The memory of every deed and act of Rachel was fresh in the old man's mind. His love was undiminished.

A beautiful courtship followed this first love of Jacob for Rachel. Rachel hurriedly told her father, Laban, of the coming of Jacob, and at his invitation he abode with them for one month. What a month that must have been—the attending Rachel as she cared for the sheep, the passing of evenings of sweet fellowship in the desert moonlight, and the enjoyment of pleasant conversations round the family hearth! At the end of the month, which passed like a day, Jacob asked Laban for the hand of his daughter and offered to serve for her for seven years as Laban's servant. Jacob could think of nothing better than living in this household as a hired servant if he could be in the presence of his beloved Rachel. The Scripture passes over those seven years in one sentence by saying, "They seemed unto him but a few days for the love he had to her." Here is scope for a great story, but it must be left to your imagination as you think of the kind of relationship that would make toil, such as that which Jacob later claimed that he endured, namely, sleep departing from him, being bitten by the frost, wandering by night and by day in order to protect the sheep, so easy that seven years seemed as seven days. Here is a demonstration of what love will enable a man to endure for a wife and for a home and for the object of his desire.

The Woman Who Commanded a Man's Love

At the end of that season, a great wrong was done to Jacob by his future father-in-law. The marriage day arrived, the great eastern feast had been enjoyed, and it was time for Jacob to take his wife, when he discovered the base trick that had been played upon him through the means of veiling these eastern women. He had been given Rachel's sister, Leah, in marriage. One wonders why Jacob did not furiously demand his rightful wife and take her away. The only explanation of Jacob's submission to this wrong was that he recognized it as retribution for his own act of cheating Esau and deceiving his aged father. Jacob was compelled to serve another seven years for Rachel. Whether he was married at the beginning or at the end of these seven years is not quite clear from the Scriptural narrative, but at length marriage came. Jacob could not get along without Rachel; so he served fourteen years of his life to possess her.

Now that marriage has occurred, we ought to look at the woman whom Jacob loved. Rachel certainly had her faults. One commentator calls her a soulless beauty, who thought only of self. We cannot agree with this, although no one can read the story of Rachel's life without recognizing her blemishes; but who is there who has not some blemishes in his character? From the beginning, Rachel was jealous of Leah, but why should she not be? She had been wronged as much by Laban's effrontery and Leah's connivance in it as had Jacob. If ever there was an argument against polygamy, it is this story. There simply could not be happiness in a household in which the affections and interests were divided between two women. As to Jacob's willingness to practice polygamy, we must make our judgment from the nature of the times in which he lived, in the lack of civil law, and from the absence of religious law upon his life. Second, Rachel was superstitious. When

Jacob and his family and hers finally left Haran for Canaan after a twenty-one years' sojourn, Rachel took her father's teraphim, or idols, with her. According to the revelation made to Abraham, to Isaac, and to Jacob concerning the true God, this was idolatry and ultimately it had to be purged from Jacob's household. Third, Rachel was petulant. God had withheld children from her, and she blamed Jacob for it. How strange that in the cases of so many mothers who had great children in the Bible their offspring were withheld from them until they reached an advanced age! Such was the case with Hannah, with the wife of Manoah, with Sarah, and with Elizabeth. One writer suggests that the purpose of this was to develop faith in them.

There were many favorable aspects to Rachel's character, as well as faults. She was not only attractive to Jacob, but she was a helpful, devoted wife under the most trying circumstances. She shared with Jacob most of his tests without complaint. There is also no shadow or stain over Rachel's virtuous life. She was an upright woman. Probably the greatest thing that can be attributed to her is that she was the mother of the mightiest of the patriarchs, who was great in faith and character, namely, Joseph. As one studies the life of Joseph and recognizes the purity of his character, he realizes that it must have had its source in his mother. When Rachel died, she was mourned by all who knew her and was crowned with many benedictions. Thus it is in the marriage ceremony that we pray, "God make you like Jacob and Rachel." No fault of Rachel diminished the love Jacob bore her. Here at least we see a wonderful figure of how Christ loves His church in spite of her faults. That means that He loves you in spite of the blemishes in your character, if you are a member of His church.

III. THEIR LIFE TOGETHER

There is only one hint of a jar in the harmonious relationship between Rachel and Jacob. The old adage says, "The course of true love never did run smooth." Sometime, somewhere, your perfect human relationship will be momentarily spoiled. This strain on the family tie was due to a commendable desire on the part of Rachel for children. Recall how the Scripture says that when Peninah, one wife of Elkanah, had children, and Hannah, another wife of Elkanah, had no children, that her adversary provoked her sorely to fret over this. Thus it was with Rachel. Her whole being was bound up in the thought of becoming a mother, and this desire ultimately became the cause of her death. To Jacob she said, "Give me children or I die." Jacob responded, "Am I in the stead of God?" and his anger was momentarily kindled against her, but it did not last long. Jacob could not continue angry with Rachel. It simply is not possible to cherish anger and reproach against one whom you love. The essence of love is that you forgive.

The time came when these two perennial lovers were to be separated by death. Here we catch the first glimpse in the Scripture of the price a woman pays for children. It is true that some because of joy that a child is born into the world refuse to admit sorrow, but terrible suffering is the lot of all women who become mothers, and some suffer even unto death. If it is true in natural life that woman must pass through the valley and the shadow of death if children are to be born, why should this not also be true in the spiritual life? It is true, for except Zion travail, her children will not be born. Converts to Christ are won through the suffering of the church. Rachel's time evidently came early, while she was traveling to Bethlehem as the Virgin Mary later did. The Scripture says, "She had hard labor." Finally, the attendant laid the little baby boy in her arms. Rachel was able to summon only enough strength to respond, "Child of my sorrow," before she passed away. This name, "Benoni," was a prophecy by Rachel of the sufferings of her people. Like a ray of faith breaking over her last moments, she looked into the future and saw what Israel and the Church must bear. Centuries later, Jeremiah heard the voice and said, "Thus saith the Lord. A voice was heard in Rama, lamentation and bitter weeping; Rachel weeping for her children and refused to be comforted for her children because they were not." When Herod slaughtered the innocents, the word of Jeremiah was again fulfilled in the crying of the mothers, and thus Rachel stands as an example of suffering motherhood before the whole world, and thus we honor her.

The effect on Jacob of the passing of Rachel was disastrous. It brought a grief from which he never fully recovered even till his death. Some people seem to be able to brush aside the loss of a loved one in a few weeks. Not so with Jacob. Jacob went about his regular duties of life, but now and then he let fall a word that revealed that he had buried his heart in that tomb on the road to Bethlehem, which remains to our present day. After the death of Rachel, Jacob transferred his love to her children, whom whenever he saw, he remembered the lovely dark-eyed daughter of Laban. Thus we hear the story of Joseph and the coat of many colors given by Jacob because of the love for him. Thus we hear the new name of Rachel's last child now called "Benjamin," or "son of my right hand," by Jacob, for by these two children Jacob now set his store. It is no wonder that a controversy arose between the ten other sons of Jacob and these two, and that when Joseph had been sold into Egypt and the ten sons had returned from their first visit to him as the unrecognized governor of Egypt, demanding that Benjamin be taken also, Jacob said, "My son shall not go down . . . if mischief befall him . . . then shall ye bring down my gray hairs with sorrow to the grave." Finally, when word came to Jacob that

The Woman Who Commanded a Man's Love 35

Joseph was still alive, the Bible says, "The spirit of Jacob their father revived and Israel said, It is enough. Joseph my son is yet alive. I will go and see him before I die." From being called Jacob, which means supplanter, we now have a man called Israel, which means the prince of God, which transformation was wrought through suffering brought to him through his love for Rachel. He had been made to limp through life because he had wrestled with an angel; he had recognized the sins of his youth returning to him in his age; and he was lifted to a life of worthiness to be the progenitor of the Christ, through love.

We only call your attention to the following lessons: First, that Jacob represents Israel dispersed and suffering and by means of suffering ultimately brought back to God. Second, Jacob may be made to represent Christ, Who loved His church to the end. What meaning this holds for every believer who is a part of His bride! Third, Benoni, or "Son of my sorrow," re-echoes in the New Testament experience of the bride of Christ. The church will have suffering in this world, but it will be united with Him in love forever. Thus it is written, "If we suffer with Him, we shall also be glorified together." Benoni will become Benjamin, "Son of my right hand."

III

THE WOMAN WHO LAUGHED AT GOD

Sarah laughed within herself.

THERE is no division of opinion concerning the name of the woman who laughed at God. It was Sarah, who is called by the Lord, "The mother of the nations of the earth." The choice of a woman who lived nearly four thousand years ago as an object of discourse is to guarantee that the ideas people hold concerning her are hazy. Nevertheless, we have considerable information concerning Sarah, which we may receive from the Bible, and that information leads us to believe that she was quite a different sort of person from that which the average person would think her to be.

The entire record of the life of Sarah is connected with the knowledge we have of Abraham. For this she is highly commended by Peter, who says, "In the old time the holy women also, who trusted in God, adorned themselves, being in subjection unto their own husbands: even as Sarah obeyed Abraham, calling him lord: whose daughters ye are, as long as ye do well." The only record we have of Sarah is that of a devoted wife throughout her entire life. She is introduced to us as the wife of Abraham, and as such she died. As the wife of her husband, she fulfills all of the demands of God's precepts. Great emphasis has been placed upon the fact that Abraham obeyed God and it was counted unto him for righteousness. He obeyed God when he left Ur of the Chaldees at the divine command in order to go out to a land he knew not. It was an adventure of faith. But we forget that Sarah also left Ur of the Chaldees along with Abraham on just as great faith and

The Woman Who Laughed At God

in just as great an adventure. In fact, it is much harder on a woman to leave her native land and kindred and friends than it is for a man to do so. For this obedience to God and her husband, Sarah should be greatly honored as a pioneer woman. Even the lineage of Sarah is traced through her husband rather than through herself. She is called "the daughter of Abraham's father but not of his mother." The common Jewish tradition accepted by Jerome and Josephus is that Sarah was the daughter of Haran, the brother of Abraham, who died in Ur of the Chaldees, and hence she would be Abraham's own niece. Thus he could refer to her as his sister, as he did on several occasions to save them both from death. Sarah shared Abraham's wanderings, which were commanded by God, his deflections due to his weakness of faith, and his great triumph that caused him to be called "the father of the faithful" and "the friend of God," until at the advanced age of one hundred twenty-seven she died and was buried in the cave of Machpelah, the only piece of ground Abraham owned in the Promised Land.

Sarah's name was originally "Sarai," which means "My Princess." This suggests two beautiful things: first, the fact that Sarah was a woman of high social standing in the country from which she came, and second, that she stood in a very endearing relationship to her husband Abraham. When we consider that Babylon, which was a later name for Ur of the Chaldees, was the center of philosophy and astronomy and culture of that ancient day, we realize that Sarah had a social standing next to none. That she should become the princess of Abraham is not unusual when we consider that the Scripture referred to her several times as "fair," "very fair," "lovely to look upon." Sarah was a woman of such beauty that wherever she journeyed, the admiring eyes of people were upon her, and she was immediately coveted for the harems of the rulers of the land, such as Pharaoh in Egypt and Abimelech in southern

Canaan. This was a section of the world in which women were noted for their beauty. One writer says concerning the women of Circassian area, "There are no cheeks so soft and creamy, no eyes so deep and lustrous as theirs, no forms so sylph-like and willowy." Sarah was also a wealthy princess, for Abraham was a prince who had much silver and gold and hundreds of armed retainers who were born in his household. All of this was at the command of Sarai.

The name of our subject was changed from Sarai, "My princess," to Sarah, at the same time that Abram's name was changed to Abraham. The adding of the syllable, or consonant, to the names of these two persons, represents JAH, or Jehovah, a symbol of the establishment of the covenant between God and Abraham's house. The sign of that covenant was circumcision. The essence of it was that God had chosen Abraham and his seed to be the progenitors of the Messiah, that He would give unto the seed of Abraham the Land of Canaan, and that God would be their God. As for Sarah, God at that time promised that He would give her a son and that she should become a mother of nations. Let us remember that not only Abraham is listed in the great roster of the heroes of the faith in the eleventh chapter of the Book of Hebrews but that Sarah also is listed. The Scripture says, "Through faith also Sarah herself received strength to conceive seed, and was delivered of a child when she was past age, because she judged Him faithful who had promised." She was one who "through faith obtained promises" and "of whom the world was not worthy." Thus when we consider Sarah we must remember that though she had shortcomings and though at times she was guilty of unbelief, nevertheless the great characteristic of her life was that of faith. In her we see a beautiful, cultured princess who because of faith in the promise of God underwent great sacrifices. She was essentially good and was among those redeemed by faith in the Lord.

The Woman Who Laughed At God

Sarah's experience illustrates the various kinds of relationship the soul can have to God, all of which may be subsumed under the word "laughter." Laughter is an art that may be developed for one's enjoyment and relaxation, or it may be a science for the sake of ridicule, mockery, and irony. One well-known writer recently made a wide research into the matter of humor and wrote a book on the science of humor, which analyzes its principles, laws, and rules for the sake of producing laughter. Our subject confines our interest to three kinds of laughter that express an attitude of the mind. We shall call them: "The Laughter of Unbelief," "The Laughter of Faith," and "The Laughter of Joy," all of which are illustrated by "The Woman Who Laughed at God," namely, Sarah.

I. THE LAUGHTER OF UNBELIEF

Sarah definitely laughed at God. Hers was the laugh of unbelief. Perhaps when we understand the entire circumstance, we shall not condemn Sarah for this act of laughing at God's promise. In the early days of the history of mankind, the Lord appeared unto men in what are called "theophanies," that is, He assumed the human form. He appeared to men and conversed with them. This is the kind of communion Adam had with the Lord. It is also the kind of communion enjoyed by Enoch, who, it says, "walked with God." Now, the Lord on several occasions appeared unto Abraham and also unto Sarah his wife. On this particular occasion, Abraham was sitting in the door of the main tent of his colony when three men came by. The community of Abraham's tribe must have been quite large, for on one occasion he mustered three hundred eighteen men who had been born in his own household and who were able to bear arms, in order to go to the rescue of Lot. The Scripture does not say how these men approached Abraham, who was sitting in the door of his tent under the oaks of Mamre. It simply says, "Lo, three men stood by him, and when he saw them he ran to meet them from the tent door and bowed himself toward the ground and said, My Lord if now I have found favor in Thy sight pass not away, I pray Thee, from Thy servant." Perhaps Abraham recognized in them the appearance of angels and of God Himself and thus insisted on extending to them hospitality. The New Testament says that "some have entertained angels unawares." Abraham knew that he was entertaining an unusual group of personages, but Sarah entertained them unawares. It is very interesting that though Sarah had all of the servants that were in the community of Abraham, she herself cooked the meal that was set before these messengers of God. It consisted of calf, butter, milk, and freshly made bread, but it was given with gladness and true hospitality.

This primitive family was now to receive its reward for entertaining angels of God. When they had finished their meal, the spokesman said, "Where is Sarah, thy wife?" Abraham replied, "Behold, in the tent." Then said the angel of the Lord, "I will return unto thee according to the time of life. Lo, Sarah, thy wife, shall have a son." For decades, Sarah and Abraham had been longing and waiting for the day when almighty God would give them a son, and now the time of life for both of them was past for such things. In fact, their desire for a son had been so keen that they had resorted to a sinful expedient in the taking of Hagar, Sarah's bondmaid, as a substitute for Sarah through whom Abraham might have children. They had finally come to the place where they believed it was not the divine purpose to give the child through Sarah but that Abraham would receive the child through another woman. This expedient had nothing but sorrow connected with it for this family. Nevertheless, in some mysterious way God had a purpose connected with it. When the Lord makes a promise to His servants, He will fulfill that promise regardless of the seeming impossibility of doing

The Woman Who Laughed At God 41

so. At this time of life for both of them, the giving of a child meant a definite creative act on the part of God. In fact, when the Lord changed Sarah's name at the institution of the covenant and promised her a son, Abraham fell upon his face and laughed out of unbelief because of the impossibility of the thing, but God reiterated the promise and said, "Sarah thy wife shall bear thee a son indeed and thou shalt call his name Isaac and I will establish My covenant with him for an everlasting covenant and with his seed after him." Now, as the angels announced these words a second time to Abraham, Sarah, who was in the tent, heard it and we read that she laughed within herself, thinking that this was absolutely impossible. Hers was the laugh of irony, the laugh of unbelief that such a promise should be reiterated when now it was impossible. The time was when the purpose for which they had left Haran could have been fulfilled, when they could have had posterity, when a new line could have been founded, but now, according to Sarah's way of thinking, it was impossible.

The laughter in Sarah was not that of an unbeliever. It was that of a believer who did not trust the divine promise. It was not that of a mocker, but it was that of one act of unbelief in the life of a believing person. It was spontaneous unbelief at the incongruity of the thing that a woman nearly one hundred years old should have a son. The essence of humor is the incongruity of a thing, and it was this that made Sarah laugh. She considered the whole situation from a purely human side and not from the divine side. In fact, as yet, Sarah did not even know that this was God who was speaking to Abraham. Only eyes of faith like those of Abraham would discern that.

The laughter of Sarah was quite unlike the laughter of unbelief when they know that they are laughing at God. Their laughter is the laughter of ridicule and hate. Such mockery has its source in basic wickedness and antipathy to God from the degeneracy of the human heart. It is akin to the mockery of Christ upon the cross, when men said unto Him, "If Thou be the Son of God, come down from the cross." This mockery is centered in the intellectualism of our day, which would confine God to natural law and to that alone and laughs at His ability to intervene in the course of natural events or to do the things that are written in the Scripture such as to perform a miracle or to foretell in prophecy the events that would take place hundreds of years later. For this reason, they brand passages in the Book of Daniel, Isaiah, and Amos as forgeries or interpolations. They laugh at the idea of a virgin birth, by which Mary could conceive a child without a human father. They laugh at the idea of the resurrection, which is so clearly proclaimed in the Bible by means of the reappearances of the same Jesus after His death and resurrection. They laugh at the inspiration of the Bible, saying that it is a mechanical theory of God dictating to man. They mock the teaching concerning the second coming of the Son of God in the clouds and glory to judge the earth and the nations, and they laugh, also, at the idea of judgment and of hell. Men say that the only hell that exists is the hell they experience now.

What a contrast this is to the kind of teaching we received in our universities some years ago. Claude M. Fuess, in writing on the life of Calvin Coolidge while he was in college, tells of one of the most loved teachers at Amherst College under whom Calvin studied. He says, "At heart and by training a devout and rather orthodox New England Congregationalist, Garman early adopted the Socratic method and a policy of setting up one theory after another, each of which he in turn demolished until he and his listeners had reached the truth. He insisted at each stage that they weigh the evidence and, through reason alone, arrive at a logical and irrefutable conclusion—Christianity. Garman published almost nothing. He was too busy teach-

The Woman Who Laughed At God

ing, but the class of 1908 placed on his tablet in the college church the words, 'He chose to write on living men's hearts.' Coolidge said of him, 'We looked upon Garman as a man who walked with God.' " Would God we had more teachers such as this in our universities today, to turn out men of honesty and fidelity, as Calvin Coolidge.

Such laughter at God and the promises and things of God leads one to inevitable sorrow and trouble. The first outcome is sin, for unbelief will blast one's faith in the values of any abiding thing in life. It will bring about an utter disregard of ethical standards, for once God is reasoned away or laughed away, all moral standards that depend upon the belief in God will be laughed away. Once you laugh at God in unbelief, you will begin to live as if there is no God. Such laughter will lead to pain. One who died by his own hand said, "How short the sin. How long the pain." Wherever there is sin and unbelief, there inevitably follows pain and ultimately death.

Bob Jones tells of an incident that occurred when he was preaching to a great southern audience about the atheistic drift in the educational life of America. A man sat on the front seat and followed every word he spoke with an expression of agony he had rarely seen upon a human face. When the service was over, his pastor said to Mr. Jones, "Did you see that man who looked like the incarnation of agony? He sat in the front seat today. He is one of the truest Christians I have ever known. He is on my board. He had one daughter. She was a beautiful child. She grew up in the Sunday-school and church. She finished high school. He sent her off to a certain college. At the end of nine months, she came home with her faith shattered. She laughed at God and the old-time religion. She broke the hearts of her father and mother. They wept over her. They prayed for her. It availed nothing. At last they chided her. She rushed upstairs, stood in front of her mirror, took a gun, and blew out her brains." That man's life has been marked with sorrow ever since. It is to this kind of pain and death that unbelief and the laughter of mockery at God leads one. As I said before, it is one thing to have an individual act of unbelief and it is another thing to take an attitude of unbelief in one's life. Sarah's laughter was only that of an individual act, and yet it was culpable.

II. THE LAUGHTER OF FAITH

The evidence from the Scripture that Sarah's life was not one of permanent unbelief is shown by her place in the roster of the heroes of the faith, when it is said that "by faith she received strength to conceive seed when she was past age." Thus Sarah exercised the faith that is pleasing to God. It is interesting that when Sarah laughed within her heart, God knew that she had laughed, for the Lord said to Abraham, "Wherefore did Sarah laugh, saying shall I of a surety bear a child when I am old? Is anything too hard for the Lord?" And then He reiterated the promise that He would now give to Abraham and Sarah a son. Very sobering is the thought here revealed that God knows the unspoken thoughts of our heart. There is no use praying for definite spiritual objects if we regard iniquity within our heart, for the Lord will not hear us. There is no use parading to the world that we believe the promises if we laugh at them secretly within our heart. All such things are known to God. Christ was able to tell men their thoughts before they ever expressed them. The Lord reads the unspoken attitudes of our heart. When Sarah heard this, she denied that she had laughed, saying, "I laughed not." Truly she had not laughed openly. She had not even so much as smiled, but in her heart, deep down, she had laughed at the incongruity of a woman of her age having a child. Christ once taught that men are guilty of adultery if they look upon a woman to lust after her in their hearts, and that they are guilty of murder if they are even angry

The Woman Who Laughed At God

with their brother. Here we see the Lord driving religion deep down into the heart, and He rebuked Sarah because she laughed secretly.

Surely when this second statement of the promise was given to Sarah and Abraham, they should have believed and not have needed the third reiteration of the divine promise. It seems that this very rebuke of the Lord for Sarah's inner unbelief caused the change in her from unbelief to faith, so that she thereafter was able to act upon the promise. It was at this time that the physical vigor of Sarah and Abraham was divinely renewed so that Sarah again became a great beauty desired by Abimelech, and Abraham continued in the vigor of manhood for the rest of his life, later having six other sons. This continuance in strength revealed that Sarah and Abraham continued in faith in accordance with the divine promise, for her New Testament record says that she judged the Lord faithful, Who had promised.

When the Lord spoke to Abraham, He said, "Is anything too hard for the Lord?" This promise of what the Lord was to perform for this aged couple reminds us of the promise and the wonderful creative act of God in connection with the Lord Jesus in His birth of a virgin. When the angel Gabriel made the great annunciation unto Mary that the child that should be born of her should be the Son of God, she asked, "How can these things be?" Gabriel replied, "With God all things are possible." It would not be a stretch of the imagination if after such a visitation of God, Abraham and Sarah had believed that Isaac was to be the Messiah. Perhaps they did.

Notable is it that the men who have done the impossible throughout the ages have been men who walked with God. The generation of Noah mocked his preaching about judgment and a flood. They ridiculed his building of a great ark, which would preserve those who believed from the judgment of the flood, but for one hundred and twenty years Noah believed God and walked with Him, and Noah accomplished the impossible.

When Moses stood before Pharaoh demanding the release of the Israelites, Pharaoh laughed and said, "Who is the God of the Israelites, that I should let the people go?" But because of Moses' faith in the Lord, he was able to deliver that people from the armies of Egypt and from the obstacles of a great wilderness; the Lord undertook for him.

When David visited the armies of Israel that were being defied by the great giant of the Philistines he said, "Who is this that defieth the God of Israel? I will go forth and fight with him," and in the name of the Lord, David stilled the mocking tongue of Goliath.

Likewise when Samson was placed in the house of Dagon to be made the object of the cruel sport and mockery of the Philistines, it was because they ridiculed the God of Samson and said that Dagon their god had delivered him into their hands that the mocking laughter of the Philistines was brought down to a howl of mourning for the thousands slain in Samson's death. With God, one man is a majority, whatever the odds he faces. It was with this in mind that the writer of the list of the heroes of the faith said, "Who through faith subdued kingdoms, wrought righteousness, obtained promises, stopped the mouths of lions, quenched the violence of fire, escaped the edge of the sword, out of weakness were made strong, waxed valiant in fight, turned to flight the enemies of the aliens. Women received their dead raised to life again. Others were tortured not accepting deliverance that they might obtain a better resurrection, of whom the world was not worthy."

Thus it is that faith laughs at the world. Instead of being defeated by the mockery and the ridicule of the world, the man of faith is one who is able to laugh at all obstacles and all difficulties that face him.

III. THE LAUGHTER OF JOY

The Scripture says, "The Lord did as He had said unto Sarah." The days came when her son was born, when the joy of the fulfilled promise belonged to Sarah. Bear in mind that on four occasions God had said to Abraham and Sarah that He would give them a son through whom the nations of the world should be blessed and that the seed of Abraham and Sarah should be as innumerable as the stars in the heavens and the sand of the seashore for multitude. Just as this expectancy had led them to an act of unbelief in reference to Hagar and to Ishmael, now this great expectation led them to joy as it was fulfilled. How long they had prayed and waited and longed for this promise to be fulfilled! Now by a supernatural act of God, it came to pass.

Sarah named her son "Isaac," which means laughter, because she said, "God hath made me to laugh so that all the world will laugh with me." Believing him to be the progenitor of the Messiah, if not the Messiah Himself, this was the laugh of salvation. It was the laugh of the joy of knowing that one's sins would be forgiven through the Man sent by God. Through this son, all the nations of the earth were to be blessed, through the tidings of salvation. How wonderfully that has all been fulfilled in the descendant of Isaac, the Lord Jesus Christ! Wherever the name of Jesus has gone, as Savior, there has been joy, joy unspeakable and full of glory, joy of sins forgiven, joy of victory, joy of the expectation of reigning with Him in the heavenlies. All this Sarah and Abraham felt when Isaac was born.

This laughter of joy was the laughter of trusting God's promise. After this Abraham was put to the test to sacrifice his son Isaac on Mount Moriah in fulfillment of the divine command. Much we have honored Abraham for the fulfillment of this act of obedience, but did Sarah have no suffering? Did she not know that Abraham had intended this? Such a relationship as Abraham and Sarah enjoyed would have prevented his hiding his purpose from her. Though it may not have been stated, nevertheless Sarah could tell by the look in his eye, by the suffering written upon his own brow, by the circumstances of his leaving with Isaac and the wood but with no lamb for the sacrifice to go to Mount Moriah. What agony of soul she must have passed through! What consecration it took for her not to stand in the way of her husband's purpose! If Abraham believed that God could raise Isaac from the dead and restore him unto him, Sarah must have believed it also, and thus we not only have in Isaac a type of the death and resurrection of the Lord Jesus Christ, but we also have a true faith on the part of these two parents in the necessary death of a divinely sent Son for salvation. The old Jewish legend stated by Josephus is that when Abraham and Isaac returned, they found Sarah dying of a broken heart. The terrible ordeal had been too much for her, and shortly after this Abraham laid her away in the cave of Machpelah, where he himself was later to be buried. The return of Isaac with his father was a vindication of the divine purposes and promises in relation to him. Sarah and Abraham had the joy of trusting God's promise.

Theirs was also the joy of salvation through the fulfillment of the promise of Christ, for what Isaac represented to them, the Lord Jesus Christ represents to us. Where Christ is not known, there is no laughter; there is no joy; there is no peace; but wherever He is known, joy follows. Truly every soul who trusts in Christ may laugh, rejoice, and sing for joy.

IV

THE WOMAN WHO WON A HUSBAND

And now, my daughter, fear not. I will do to thee all that thou requirest, for all the city of my people doth know that thou art a virtuous woman.

THIS pastoral idyl begins with the statement, "When the judges ruled Israel." The period of the Judges recalls the storm and stress of Israel's history. It is hardly possible to imagine that this beautiful pastoral scene should have taken place in the period described in the Book of Judges. Here we see a quiet scene of family life, of bereavement, of migration, of poverty and of blessing, which has been designated as one of the most excellent in literature, and in no way suggests the wild, stormy period of the Judges. Here, in this story of Ruth, is beauty, love, and truth exquisitely presented.

In this story, we have all the lights and the shadows of human life presented. When Naomi returned from Moab, she said to her companions in Bethlehem, "Call me not Naomi. Call me Mara, for the Lord hath dealt very bitterly with me." Naomi means "blessedness." Mara means "bitterness." These are the two aspects of human life, and they are found in the Book of Ruth, for it begins with sorrow and it ends with happiness. Thus it is that satisfaction and discontent, hope and disappointment, achievement and failure, joy and sorrow, follow every man and every woman through life.

It is said that this story of the heartaches and the joys of a humble family can hardly be placed in the time of the Judges, yet how little one would think if he read the headlines of the papers of our day that quiet church, family, and business life continue anywhere. The Book of Judges concerns itself with the headlines of four hundred and fifty years of history of Israel, whereas the Book of Ruth concerns itself with one generation. It is the contrast of flying over a great series of mountain ranges by aeroplane and of living in a quiet, green valley. In the valley, life moves slowly, with the lowing of the herd and the bleating of the sheep, the growing of the oaks and the flowing of the river. Flying through the sky, life moves over great sections as the valleys pass under one's view. So it is in the Bible. It deals with the history of nations and cosmic movements, but it also occupies its attention with the life of human beings as such. It is an error for us to occupy our attention with either exclusively.

The events of the period of Judges are equal in length to the history of America from its earliest times to the present. Think of trying to encompass the history of the great leaders of America for this long period of time in a few pages so as to designate the general tenor of American life. Like as in the Book of Judges, hideous sins of murder, war, civil struggle, oppression, and depression would follow each other successively. In Judges we read of Gideon, Jephthah, Barak, Samson, Shamgar, Ehud, and other mighty men who performed great deeds. We read of hideous scenes of immorality, of pillage, of murder, of oppression, and of wickedness. We read of periods of rising in spiritual life and again of falling on the part of the people, periods of prosperity and periods of depression, but the one clause that describes it all is that "every man did what was right in his own eyes." That standard is quite comparable to that of our own day, which is individualistic, in which men have rejected any external standard of righteousness and do what is right in their own eyes. In this stormy, wild period was the simple, beautiful story before us now.

The narrative opens with an economic depression in which a seemingly good family was caught, much to its

The Woman Who Won a Husband 51

sorrow. There are certain cosmic movements in the world in which the righteous suffer with the wicked, in which it is not always a man's fault when he is down and out. Because a man suffers, one should not judge him as a greater sinner than someone else, for in these national or cosmic movements, the rain falls upon the righteous and upon the wicked indiscriminately. Because of this depression, which had resulted from a famine in the land, the family of Elimelech, which included his wife Naomi and his two sons Mahlon and Chilion, departed from the land of Judah to go to Moab. Either Elimelech was discouraged with the conditions that existed under the Judges or else out of unbelief he left his inheritance, to miss the chastement of the Lord by going into another land, especially a land that was under the condemnation of the Lord.

Hence our story opens in the Land of Moab. We want you to know how Ruth won a husband. And we want you to know the typical meaning of Ruth.

I. The Story of Ruth

No sooner had the little family arrived in Moab than Elimelech, the father, took sick and soon died. It was a hard blow that struck Naomi, but its strength was lessened by the fact that she had two stalwart, faithful sons by her side. Happiness, which seemed so fleeting and elusive to this little family, now appeared to return again for a brief time, for the two sons found for themselves wives of the women of Moab. Chilion married a woman named Orpah, and Mahlon married Ruth. The unified household dwelt together for ten years, and then misfortune visited again, for the angel of death was hovering around the once desolate home, and this time it summoned both Mahlon and Chilion. Poor Naomi now lost the last prop upon which she had leaned. The light of prosperity was gone, and gloom enveloped the sorrowing old woman.

Then, as happens so often in the lives of those of advanced years, she began to think of her old home, of her people and of her nation. She heard that the Lord had visited His people and had given them bread, and following her thoughts she turned her face toward Judea. Stating her determination to her daughters, she urged them both to tarry in Moab, where they might find rest with their own people and in their fathers' houses. Orpah accepted the advice and departed, but Ruth remained with Naomi and determined to return with her to Judea. One can well imagine what a change must have occurred in the little town during the time that Naomi was gone. The houses perhaps were the same and the streets were the same, but many of her old companions were now gone. The famine had taken its toll, and the community cemetery had many new markers. Yet there were enough old friends there to greet her and to recognize the great difference in her. Instead of being in the bloom of womanhood, she now was old, bent, gray, wrinkled, and sorrowful, so that they even said, "Can this be Naomi?" Acknowledging that she was the same, she asked them to call her Mara, which means bitterness, because of her sorrow.

But Naomi was not alone, for Ruth had determined to go with her, and she became the only comfort Naomi had in her return. Together these two lovely women, who were very fond of one another, determined to face their trials bravely and in mutual forbearance. Hence, there is no implication of any complaint made one to another, nor is there ever any chiding or any spirit of strife. If love exists between women, which is beautiful, here is one of the highest of all. Here was one, not of mother and daughter, but of mother-in-law and daughter-in-law, which transcends even the best of blood relationship. Ruth urged her mother-in-law to allow her to go and to work as a gleaner in the harvest, and finally Naomi acceded to the request and allowed her to go. Through her work, Ruth became acquainted with the owner of the field in which she happened to be gleaning. After many kindnesses, which manifested the concern and the heart interest of the owner of the field, Boaz, for Ruth, Ruth appealed to him as a kinsman redeemer to marry her. To this Boaz responded. The marriage was performed in the gate of the city of Bethlehem. Ruth and Naomi were taken to his home, and before long a little life made its advent into the world, by name Obed; so that the women of Bethlehem sang and praised Naomi, saying that her daughter-in-law, Ruth, had been better to her than seven sons and that the Lord through her had restored Naomi's life and nourished her old age.

As one reads and rereads this story, the outstanding characteristic of it is the recognition of the Lord. The Lord is given the central place by all characters in the narrative. First, Naomi, being most prominent, draws our attention. She is the one who suffered most, and yet everything that came to her in the lights and shadows of her life was of the Lord. When loss after loss struck the little home in Moab until Naomi was left desolate of her husband and her two sons, she confessed to her daughters-in-law that all of this had been of the Lord. In her solemn plea to both of them to turn back to their fathers' houses because of the darkness and gloom of the outlook, she said, "For it grieveth me much for your sakes that the hand of the Lord is gone out against me." Later when Naomi returned to Bethlehem, she said to her friends and companions, "The Almighty hath dealt very bitterly with me. I went out full and the Lord hath brought me home again empty," and "Why then call ye me Naomi seeing the Lord hath testified against me and the Almighty hath afflicted me?" Evidently Naomi here confessed that she had been the moving spirit in the migration of the family from Bethlehem to Moab, and she recognized that everything was of the Lord. It is even written that she acknowledged that the end of the famine in Bethlehem was due to the Lord, for she said that the Lord had visited His people in giving them bread. This reinforces the belief that it was because of an act of unbelief on the part of Naomi that the little family went to Moab. And, finally, in Naomi's life, we have the recognition that their good fortune and their restoration and their blessing were of the Lord.

Similarly, Ruth placed the Lord central in the whole of her life. She had been born and brought up in a country where the god Chemosh was worshiped, to whom human sacrifices were given and under whose worship the nation had degenerated into a group of licentious people indulging every physical whim, but when she learned of the Lord, she rejected Chemosh, the idol, and chose the Lord as her God. This decision we shall examine a little later, and it was of great religious value, a true conversion of Ruth. Later we find that the narrative says, "It was her hap to light upon the field of Boaz." Here is definite implication of the place of Providence in Ruth's life. Many are the fortuitous occurrences in the lives of us all, which begin a chain of events leading to some great crisis in our lives. God plays a part in the smallest things of our lives. Ruth also obeyed Naomi in the Lord. She recognized that she was now serving Naomi's God, and in the smallest things she followed the desires of her mother, Naomi.

Likewise Boaz put the Lord first in his life. When he came from Bethlehem to his reapers, he said to them in greeting, "The Lord be with you." They answered him, "The Lord bless thee." Whether it was the famine or religion that had taught them, these men recognized that their prosperity was of the Lord. Likewise, when Boaz discovered Ruth working in his field and had addressed her, he said, "The Lord recompense thy work and a full reward be given thee of the Lord God of Israel under Whose wings thou art come to trust." Boaz recognized Ruth's choice of coming to Judah as a religious choice of the Lord as her God, and he believed that the Lord would recompense her.

The Woman Who Won a Husband

Moreover, when Ruth ultimately settled upon him as the kinsman redeemer rather than some younger man, he said to her, "Blessed be thou of the Lord, my daughter, for thou hast showed more kindness in the latter end than at the beginning." Everything for Boaz was either of the Lord or for the Lord.

Similarly, even the people placed the Lord central in their thought and in their speech. When Boaz brought this girl to the gates of the city in order that he might take her as his wife before the people, they cried, "The Lord make the woman that is come into thy house like Rachel and Leah, which two did build the house of Israel." Only under the Lord could Boaz in the eyes of the people have the blessing upon his own house through this woman. Finally, when Obed was born, the people said unto Naomi, "Blessed be the Lord which hath not left thee this day without a kinsman that His name may be famous in Israel." It was God who had heard Naomi's prayer, and it was God who had sent the kinsman redeemer to her. Thus even the story itself is centered upon the Lord, for the descendant of Obed was none other than David, who was to be the progenitor of Christ, for David said, "The Lord said to my lord, sit thou upon my right hand until I make thy foes thy footstool." Everything in the story of Ruth centers about the Lord.

Ruth had a beautiful conversion to the Lord. I suppose that in a nominal way she had embraced the Lord as the object of her worship during the time when Naomi's two sons were still living. Here is a case of the faith of the husband sanctifying the wife and leading her into the true religion, but the day came when that sympathy toward the religion of her husband had to become a reality, for she was faced with a choice between two kinds of life. Moab offered her security, rest, and perhaps a new husband through her own people and her father's house. In Israel she had nothing to look forward to but strangers, possible poverty, the burden of supporting the aged Naomi, work by her hands, and loneliness from all of her friends and her people. It was no small decision on the part of Ruth to follow the still, small voice that led her on in the pathway of duty, of love, and of faith instead of following the way Orpah took of personal satisfaction and ease.

We are not to think that the influence of Naomi was slight in this matter. It is a great truth that the personal influence of believers does more to lead men to Christ than their words. Naomi had passed through a harrowing time of sorrow and trial, but even in the midst of all she demonstrated the validity of her faith in God, and this faith and this God commended themselves to Ruth. Ruth not only had conceived a mighty love for her mother-in-law, which was able to make her willing to support her in her old age, but she made a choice of Naomi's God. As the three of them stood out on the west of Moab's hills before they descended into the Jordan Valley that should ultimately lead over into Judah, Naomi said, "Go, return each to her mother's house: the Lord deal kindly with you, as ye have dealt with the dead, and with me. The Lord grant you that ye may find rest, each of you in the house of her husband." Then Naomi kissed them, and they all wept. It was a sad hour. Both of the girls rose to the occasion and said, "Surely we will return with thee unto thy people." But again Naomi told them to turn again and to go to their fathers' houses. Orpah kissed her mother-in-law and left. For the third time, Naomi addressed Ruth and said, "Behold, thy sister-in-law is gone back unto her people and unto her gods: return thou after thy sister-in-law." The emphasis here upon gods of Moab and the God of the Israelites reveals that this was a distinctly religious decision. Ruth then uttered the words for which she has become immortal: "Entreat me not to leave thee or to return from following after thee: for whither thou goest, I will go; and where thou lodgest I will lodge: thy people shall be my

The Woman Who Won a Husband

people, and thy God my God: where thou diest, will I die, and there will I be buried: the Lord do so to me, and more also, if aught but death part thee and me."

Hereafter the Lord was to be Ruth's God. She had passed her crisis. She had turned unto the Lord. She was truly converted. She had made the decision and was lifted into a place where a divine kinsman redeemer would be available for her.

II. How Ruth Won a Husband

Ruth was not distinguished for her beauty, but for her character. Others such as Eve, Sarah, Rebekah, and Rachel were famed because the Bible says they were fair to look upon, but never once is this said concerning Ruth. It may well be that Ruth was a comely person, but there is no hint of beauty in the Bible concerning her. We cannot even think that Ruth was young. She had been married for ten years to Mahlon and now was a widow. Yet when Ruth came to the fields of Boaz to glean after his reapers, his eye, which was accustomed to the flotsam and jetsam of Bethlehem and Judea, was able to pick her out among the gleaners in his field. Something about her bearing, her modesty, her demeanor, was different from that of the other women. He was led to ask the chief of his reapers, "Whose damsel is this?" And then it was that he heard the story of all that Ruth had done for Naomi and because of her belief in Naomi's God.

The ancient Israelites, under the law of God, had a very beautiful custom of allowing a provision to be made for the poor. It was contrary to divine law for men to reap the corners of their field or to beat their fruit-trees twice or to gather up the materials that had fallen from the reapers. This must be left for the poor. Hence, the poor followed the reaper in the fields, gleaning and gathering up what they could. They also plucked the fruit that was not ripe at the time of the first beating of the trees, and they took their little produce from the corners of the field left unreaped. It was in this activity that Ruth was now engaged when she fell under the interest of Boaz. It should be remembered that by law, when a man died leaving a widow and no children to carry on his name in the tribe, his nearest kinsman was required to marry his widow, and the first-born child of the new marriage was to take the name of the dead man in order that no family should perish out of the tribes of Israel. This was called the law of a kinsman redeemer. Boaz was a near kinsman to Naomi and hence was also a near kinsman to Ruth, and according to the law it was her right to demand this privilege from Boaz.

But Boaz demonstrated his heart interest in Ruth long before she ever made any claim to his part as a kinsman redeemer. He told her that she could freely reap after the young men and that they would not bother her in that rather violent period when a woman's virtue was not of much value and that she could drink of the water the young men had drawn. He also invited her to come and eat at his table during the season of rest. Then he commanded the young men to allow some handfuls to fall on purpose for her. When Ruth asked him, "Why have I found grace in thine eyes that thou shouldest take knowledge of me, seeing I am a stranger?" Boaz replied, "It has been fully shown me all that thou hast done unto thy mother-in-law since the death of thine husband." Boaz' interest in Ruth had been due to her character. She had a fine reputation. Later he said to her, "All the city of my people know that thou art a virtuous woman." They knew that she was a woman who had chosen the Lord. She had become a convert to Israel's God. They knew that with great care she had taken an interest in the aged Naomi, willing to work to keep her in food. They knew that she had sacrificed every comfort of life in order to return to this land with her mother-in-law. She had left her father and her mother and the land of her nativity and had come to a strange people.

The Woman Who Won a Husband 59

Boaz also learned that she was a willing worker. His chief of the reapers said, "She has continued among the gleaners even from morning until now except that she tarried a little in the house." From early morning until nearly noon, Ruth worked with only a little rest, and that trip to the house was probably due to the fact that she was unaccustomed to the difficult work of gleaning in the field. Here was a woman who was not too proud to work, and when she did not have much, she was willing to take less in order that she might keep alive.

Boaz learned that she was an obedient daughter, for her actions in some cases could only have been instigated by Naomi, and thus she was only performing Naomi's will. No wonder that the women said of Ruth, "She is better to thee than seven sons." She was fulfilling one of the original commandments.

The outcome of the matter was very happy. At the instigation of Naomi, Ruth ultimately made her claim on Boaz for a kinsman redeemer. She said, "Spread thy skirt over thy daughter, for thou art a near kinsman to me." This was a plea for marriage. The circumstances of the event reveal that Boaz' affection had already been claimed by the woman, and he was more than willing to perform the duty. He, in turn, demonstrated his wisdom and his care in order that his own name should be irreproachable and that Ruth might soon find rest. In accordance with the custom of the day, he went immediately following the harvest to the gate of the city where the elders of the people must pass by. There this righteous and just man sought out his own relative who was a nearer kinsman to Ruth than himself and asked him if he would do the kinsman duty to Ruth, for he had the privilege first of all of purchasing Mahlon's land and of raising up a posterity to Mahlon's name. This kinsman refused the duty because it would mar his own inheritance and asked Boaz to take the responsibility upon himself. Then it was that Boaz declared his intention to buy all of Elimelech's and Chilion's and Mahlon's land out of the hand of Naomi, which would make her a wealthy woman, and to take Ruth the Moabitess to be his wife and to raise up the name of the dead upon his inheritance. This generous act was applauded by the people, who in turn became witness to the marriage there in the gate and invoked the divine blessing upon them, that they might become as Rachel and Leah were to Jacob, building the house of Israel. The results of this union were that a son was born of which Naomi became the nurse and Ruth the mother, and which son in turn was the progenitor of Christ, who was the Savior of Ruth's own soul through her decision.

III. The Typical Meaning of Ruth

I suppose we could stop this sermon here, but we cannot without mentioning the remarkable typology contained in this book. There is a typical meaning to all of the characters that ought to be recognized, because it bears a vital truth for the individual Christian.

Naomi undoubtedly is typical of Israel, who in unbelief was dispersed among the heathen, passing through trial and sorrow and suffering, but ultimately recognizing that the chastenment was of the Lord and thereby repenting and returning to the land of Israel, accompanied by a believing and redeemed church, called out from among the heathen that both might be blessed through a kinsman Redeemer. The place of Israel today is the place of Naomi in Moab under chastenment, under fire and suffering and trial. When will the Israelites see that they went out full but the Lord has brought them back empty? When will they turn in repentance unto the Lord? It is their only hope. There were the Moabite women, Orpah and Ruth. Moab was a degenerate people, the individuals of whom were not allowed to stand in the congregation of the Lord to the tenth generation. God's judgment was upon them. They represent the heathen world—the Gentiles—and Orpah is typical of the unbelieving heathen who have had an opportunity to accept the knowledge of the true God and who continue in unbelief. Ruth, however, represents the Gentile church called out of heathenism, responding unto the message of the true God and opening her heart unto the gospel of grace. In Ruth we see a picture of the church as the New Testament describes it, redeemed and prepared to be the bride of the Redeemer.

Boaz represents the Redeemer, the Lord Jesus Christ, the mighty man of spiritual wealth, the one who can raise up the name of the dead upon his inheritance. He is the one for whom God has prepared the church, and He will be married to the church in mystical union, thus becoming a kinsman Redeemer to it and the restorer of Israel's life, for when Christ is married to the church, Israel will be restored to spiritual life. Israël is now in blindness and in unbelief, but when Christ and the church are married, Israel will receive benefit. All that Boaz did for Ruth is typical of what Christ has done for the church.

The events of the wedding in the gate in the midst of all of the people is typical of the great wedding feast of the Lamb. The great Book of Ephesians says that "Christ also loved the church and gave Himself for it that He might sanctify and cleanse it with the washing of water by the Word, that He might present it to Himself a glorious church, not having spot or wrinkle or any such thing, but that it should be holy and without blemish . . . this is a great mystery, but I speak concerning Christ and the church."

The church must be differentiated from all of the other saved of the ages. John the Baptist did not call himself the bride or the bridegroom, but the friend of the bridegroom. He watched the bridegroom come for the bride. Thus all of the saved of the Old Testament dispensation and those in other ages will be witnesses of the wedding, of the marriage of the Lamb and the bride. It was for this purpose that Christ died for the church that He might make it perfect in holiness and ultimately take it unto Himself. The Bible also says that this marriage feast of the Lamb is to be held in the heavenlies, for the day is coming when the heavens will open and the Lamb of God will return to receive His bride and take her away to the great wedding feast. The Bible describes this as saying, "And I heard as it were a great voice of a multitude and as the voice of many waters and of the voice of mighty thunderings, saying, Hallelujah, for the Lord God omnipotent reigneth. Let us make glad and rejoice and give honor to Him for the marriage of the Lamb is come and His wife hath made herself ready. And to her was granted that she should be arrayed in fine linen, clean and white, for the fine linen is the righteousness of the saints. And he saith unto me, Write, blessed are they which are called unto the marriage supper of the Lamb." Happy is the man who will have part in that great wedding supper of the Lamb. The entire Book of Ephesians was written to define the destiny of the church. The church is to be the peculiar and particular inheritance of the Lord Jesus Christ. It is to share His glory in the ages to come.

What a privilege, then, to participate in membership in the church of the living God! This depends upon being saved and purified now through the blood of the Lamb. In the company of the redeemed are various groups, such as an innumerable company of angels, the general assembly and church of the firstborn, and the spirits of just men made perfect. The only way to become a member of the church is to be born again. "Except a man be born again he cannot see the kingdom of God." Every born-again person is a member of the church of Jesus Christ and part of His bride to participate in the glories that are to come. He also may live today under the protection of the kinsman Redeemer. Every person stands either in the relationship of Orpah or of Ruth or of Naomi to Christ. If you are a

The Woman Who Won a Husband

Jew in unbelief, you are as Naomi was in the Land of Moab. If you are an unbeliever, a Gentile, you are as Orpah, who was rejecting the light. If you are a believer, you are as Ruth, or one who has been converted to the kinsman Redeemer.

Perhaps you have never made your decision, and now is the hour for you to choose your Redeemer. Remember the words of Ruth, "Thy God shall be my God. Thy people shall be my people. Where thou dwellest I will dwell." Can you say that? Is the God of the Christians your God? Are the Christians your people? Are you dwelling in the heavenly places now? Have you chosen the Lord? Are you willing to leave all for a kinsman Redeemer Who will break your bonds of sin and servitude and lift you to freedom and rest in the kingdom of God? Do you know what it means to have mystical union with Christ now and the promise of full union hereafter as His bride to share with Him in ruling the universe? This is all your privilege and your opportunity, but it rests with you. Choose you. Will you have the world's one Lover? Will you be pure and spotless and worthy of being espoused? He will redeem you by His own precious blood now. You may then be presented to Him without spot and without wrinkle in holiness and love.

V

THE WOMAN WHOSE SON WAS GREATEST OF MEN

> *Among them that are born of women there hath not arisen a greater than John the Baptist; notwithstanding he that is least in the kingdom of God is greater than he.*

GREATNESS is a very indefinite thing. Whether one is great or not depends upon the standard by which he is judged. Individuals may be divided in their opinion upon the greatness of a man. It seems, however, that the men of the generation of John the Baptist and those of every generation since have acknowledged that he was great.

The standard of greatness in the case of John is set by God, Who knows what is in man, Who knows the motives, the thoughts, and the desires of the human heart and Who cannot be mistaken. It was the Son of God Who said that "among them that are born of women, there hath not arisen a greater than John the Baptist." John's magnanimous character, his wonderful achievement, and his flawless courage give him this place as the greatest of those born of women. Without this evaluation by Christ, we probably would not pick John out as the greatest of men. Some of us in looking at Biblical history would decide upon Moses because of his great task of leading the children of Israel out of bondage. Others would decide upon Elijah, because he reformed the nation of Israel and preserved the true religion, the worship of Jehovah. Others would decide upon Jeremiah, because of his tremendous courage in a time of decadency and because of his great international vision. Others would even go so far back as the time of

The Woman Whose Son Was Greatest Of Men 65

Abraham and call the "father of the faithful" the greatest born of women. If we were to evaluate the life of John the Baptist from human standpoints, we would almost say that he was a failure. John left no permanent movement. He left no dynasty. He did not even found a system of thought. Seemingly he died a failure, unaccepted, and a martyr. Yet outside of the kingdom of God, John the Baptist was the greatest of those born of women.

Can it be that John the Baptist surpasses all of the great men of history who were outside the kingdom of God? Think of the military heroes from the time of Leonidas at the Battle of Marathon to Napoleon, including in that long list Alexander, Pompey, Hannibal, Julius Caesar, Genghis Khan, Charlemagne. Here were men who changed the course of nations. They seemed to be the turning-point of history. The biographers of history have called them great. Is it true that John the Baptist, about whom no biography was ever written, is greater than these? Think of the cultural leaders of the earth from the time of Pericles, with the host of outstanding men who were gathered about him during the Golden Age of Greece down to the time of the Victorian Era, and the cluster of great names that were assembled in that period, including all the courts from Constantine to Louis XIV, which came in the interim period. Was John the Baptist greater than the men who were the centers around which these cultural periods revolved? Think again of the philosophers from the time of Seneca to Immanuel Kant, including Plato, Aristotle, Philo, Plotinus, Anselm, Aquinas, Occam, Locke, Descartes, Spinoza, and Hume. Great as were all of these personages, none can compare with the son of the woman about whom we speak, that is, on the plane of divine judgment. He excelled them all.

Wherever we find a great man in history, his greatness will be largely due to the greatness of a mother who went before him. In the Granary Burying Ground, next to our church, there is a monument to the mother and father of Benjamin Franklin, a woman who had thirteen children and who trained them in the fear of God and in the honor of thrift. Who can say that the greatness of Benjamin Franklin was not due to his mother? Once when the mother of George Washington was told of the promise of little George, she said, "George is a good boy." She had inculcated in him the sense of loyalty, of humility, and of value that caused him to choose between a road of ease and one of sacrifice for the sake of his country. Even Abraham Lincoln said, "All that I am I owe to my own mother." Whenever God wished to produce a man who would be great in His eyes, He always prepared a mother first. That is why in so many cases the great men of the world have been children of old age. The women have been prepared through years of waiting, of prayer, and of meditation until ultimately God gave them the desire of their hearts. Witness the case of the aged Sarah and the birth of Isaac, of Rachel and the birth of Joseph, of the wife of Manoah and the birth of Samson, of Hannah and the birth of Samuel, and of Elisabeth and the birth of John.

This woman, Elisabeth, was a true daughter of Aaron in the time of Caiaphas, which designated a very degenerate period. Sholam Ashe, in his book, *The Nazarene*, is very accurate in his description of the hatred with which Caiaphas was held by the people because of the wickedness of the high priesthood and also of his exploitation of the masses of the people. Caiaphas set the standard for many of the lesser priests, but this daughter of Aaron was one of true piety and of devout heart. She was a woman who had long prayed for a child but who had been denied the desire of her heart. Thus she was under a reproach in Israel because she was childless. Elisabeth was one whose life was bound up in the Lord's work. She believed all the prophecies about the Messiah and also about the forerunner of the Messiah, Who would first come before the advent of the Son of God. Like the devout mothers of Israel, she longed that she might have a child and that that child should at least be the forerunner, if not the Messiah Himself. Yet as the years passed, the hopelessness of the dream bore itself in upon her, and she devoted herself utterly to the Lord's work and to that alone.

When John came, however, Elisabeth communicated to her child all of her hopes and dreams and aspirations. She poured her own life into him through training and teaching until he knew the Scriptures and the great hopes as well as she herself. Not only did this child have an annunciation in a supernatural way concerning his future, but Elisabeth fulfilled every instruction that was given to her and every requirement concerning one who might be the forerunner of the King. Because of what Elisabeth did, which enabled her son to become the greatest of men, she stands supreme among the mothers of history with the exception, of course, of the mother of our Lord. In our consideration of this woman, we invite your attention to three topics: first, Elisabeth and Mary; second, Elisabeth and John; third, Elisabeth and Jesus.

I. Elisabeth and Mary

The birth narratives of John the Baptist and of Jesus are closely intertwined in the Scripture so that no separation between them is possible. It is necessary when we are talking about one of them to talk also about the other. This interconnection is found in the story included in the first chapter of Luke's Gospel.

The father of John the Baptist was Zacharias, a priest, who served his course in the Temple, performing the daily sacrifice of incense on the golden altar before the veil. He was a godly man, who walked blameless according to the law, who fulfilled his duty, and whose practice was the incarnation of the requirements of the Mosaic Law. To this man, Almighty God sent the angel Gabriel, who appeared to him while he was burning incense and offering prayer upon the altar at the evening hour of sacrifice. Zacharias was greatly troubled but received this reply, "Fear not, Zacharias: for thy prayer is heard; and thy wife Elisabeth shall bear thee a son, and thou shalt call his name John." This greatest of all angels then proceeded to inform Zacharias of the greatness of the child in the sight of the Lord, of the manner of his life and of the ministry which he should perform. Said he, "He shall go before Him in the spirit and power of Elias, to turn the hearts of the fathers to the children, and the disobedient to the wisdom of the just; to make ready a people prepared for the Lord." Zacharias then responded, "Whereby shall I know this? for I am an old man, and my wife well stricken in years." This was doubt on the part of Zacharias and because of it Gabriel commanded that he should be dumb until the word was fulfilled. This judgment on Zacharias was a sign unto both him and to his wife that the Lord would perform His Word. As soon as Zacharias' course was finished, he returned to his home in the hill country of Judah and remained there until the birth of John the Baptist.

One might very well use his historical imagination to know what occurred in the house of Zacharias and Elisabeth in the days preceding the birth of John the Baptist. With the full knowledge of the annunciation, and with the proof in the coming of Mary, who had also seen the angel Gabriel, these devout parents must have turned to the Old Testament Scriptures and read and reread the prophecies both of the Messiah and of His forerunner, treasuring them in their hearts. Then came the day when the happy event of John's appearance to the world occurred. Within a week, all the relatives gathered together for the service of circumcision and naming the child. They insisted that he should be called after his father, Zacharias, but Elisabeth clung to the name "John." Therefore, they decided that the father would settle the matter and they asked him. He, taking a

The Woman Whose Son Was Greatest Of Men 69

tablet, wrote the name "John," which means "the grace of God." Immediately the lips and tongue of Zacharias were opened and he spoke in the words of a poem which he composed during the time of his dumbness, celebrating the wonders of God and of the child who was now born. This is called "The Benedictus"; it emphasizes the fact that God has visited and redeemed His people and raised up a horn of salvation for them to give the remission of sins through the tender mercy of God. "The Dayspring from on high hath visited us, to give light to them that sit in darkness and in the shadow of death, to guide our feet into the way of peace." This aged couple knew, and many of their friends in the hill country of Judea knew, that God had begun the redemptive process.

The faith of Elisabeth was demonstrated in this series of events. First, we have the joy with which she received the glad tidings from Zacharias that the angel of God had visited him and announced the birth of a son. There is no record of the fact that she doubted the angel's word. Rather it immediately came to pass according to the word of the angel in her life. Within five months, Mary visited at her home in Judah, and as her cousin came into her presence, both women bearing these two wonderful sons, she greeted her with an outburst of song inspired by the Holy Ghost, saying, "Blessed art thou among women, and blessed is the fruit of thy womb. And whence is this to me, that the mother of my Lord should come to me? . . . for there shall be a performance of those things which were told her of the Lord." There was no jealousy in Elisabeth's nature. She did not wonder why the Lord did not send the Messiah instead of the forerunner through her, why she was not chosen instead of Mary. Instead she pronounced the blessedness of Mary, exalted her, and strengthened her faith by her own confidence in the fulfillment of the divine promise. What a source of joy and strength and of blessing these two women were to each other during these three months in their lives can well be imagined! Moreover, Elisabeth was very faithful to the orders she had received from the angel through Zacharias concerning John's name, concerning the environment and training he should receive as a child, and concerning his teaching. He was dedicated to the Lord as a Nazarite. He should not touch strong drink and, like Samson, I suppose that a razor did not come upon his head. He was separated unto the Lord from the time of his birth, and he was filled with the Holy Ghost from before his birth, in all of which things we see the faith of Elisabeth in the infinite God.

The early life of John the Baptist was under the leadership and guidance of Elisabeth. He lived in that simple home in the hill country of Judah. Though Zacharias was probably away at Jerusalem at times in the performance of his duties as priest, nevertheless Elisabeth carried on the work in the home, bearing the responsibility of training this wonderful child. Happy childhood days mean more in one's life than almost anything else, and what days John must have spent in this godly family as they read to him the Torah, as they prayed together, and as they instructed him in the greatness of the task that was before him. Undoubtedly the later preaching of John was all due to the teaching of these parents. We read that the boy was filled with the Spirit from his birth and that he waxed strong in spirit. Under the tutelage of his mother he grew in the Spirit. There was an enlargement of his soul. Though he was filled with the Spirit from birth, nevertheless as he grew in manhood, his capacity for the Spirit was enlarged. Then he was in the desert until the day of his showing unto Israel. What a renunciation this must have been on the part of his mother, to allow him to leave and go into the desert for fasting and prayer and meditation, to live the life of a Nazarite! There, with special food of honey and wild locusts, with the pure air and the strong sunshine, his brown, clean body developed with his mind. There the Spirit Who was within him permitted him to commune with God, and there the message instilled by his own mother and announced by the angel was developed under the guidance of God. John was sent from his mother's care to do the will of God regardless of what that should cost.

II. ELISABETH AND JOHN

Just as when Jacob was an old man and had been separated long from his beloved wife, Rachel, he looked at Joseph and Benjamin and in them saw the image of his much loved wife, so whenever God looked upon John the Baptist He must have seen Elisabeth, the devout, sanctified woman of Israel. When John was in the forefront of the Christian ministry, Elisabeth was there with him. Thus it was that Susannah Wesley stood in thousands of churches in England and Nancy Hanks was in the White House of the United States, not personally, but represented in their sons.

The ministry of John the Baptist began with his showing unto Israel as the preparatory servant of the Lord. First, there was his message, which was given to the multitudes who came. He preached "Repent, for the kingdom of heaven is at hand." In that message of repentance, he told them to bring forth fruits meet for repentance because the judgment of God was impending. He said to the publican, "Exact no more than that which is appointed you;" to the soldier, "Do violence to no man, neither accuse any falsely, and be content with your wages"; to the people, "He that hath two coats, let him impart and give to him that hath none"; to the Pharisees, "The axe is laid to the root of the tree, and every tree which bringeth forth not good fruit is hewn down and cast into the fire." Though he had spoken much of repentance and of judgment, he also spoke much of mercy and forgiveness. His message was, "Behold the Lamb of God, Who taketh away the sin of the world." This message is the heart of Christianity, the message of the cross, the message of Calvary, the message of Easter, the message of redemption. John saw his successor, the Lord Jesus, as the Savior of the world. He proclaimed the Messiah, for he said, "There cometh one mightier than I after me, the latchet of whose shoes I am not worthy to unloose. He shall baptize you with the Holy Ghost and with fire." John acknowledged that the person of Christ was utterly without sin, for he said, "I have need to be baptized of you, and comest Thou to me?" He recognized also that his great work was to be that of the King of a spiritual kingdom. This mighty message to the people aroused enthusiasm and faith on the part of the multitude. They were ready to prepare themselves for the coming of the Messiah. When the religious leaders came to John and examined his message and questioned him as to whether he was the Messiah, whether he was Elias, or whether he was Jeremias, or on what authority he performed his baptism, John gave them a scathing message, calling them a "generation of vipers," telling them that God would cast them off and raise up children of stones to Abraham. He seemed to sense that these Sadducees and Pharisees would reject the Lord Jesus Christ and in anticipation he spoke the message of judgment. Then, to the chief ruler of the land, Herod, John fearlessly gave a message of correction and criticism. He told him that it was not lawful for him to have to wife the woman of his own brother. He denounced this as a great sin against the moral and spiritual law. Thereby he incurred the wrath of Herod and also of Herodias, which was ultimately to cause his own death. In this mighty ministry to the multitude, to the ecclesiastical, religious people and also to the civil powers, John revealed something of his greatness.

John was also great in personal faith, and this personal faith had been inspired in him through his own mother's knowledge of the Lord. His mother told him that the Messiah would be born shortly after him, that he was to prepare the hearts of the people by preaching repentance and turning them unto God, but when the Messiah would appear John did not know. All he knew was that God had given him a sign that when he saw the Holy Spirit descend upon a man in the form of a dove, that was the Lord. Hence, when John was baptizing the Lord Jesus Christ, and the heavens opened and the dove descended, or at least the Spirit descended as a dove, and when a voice was heard, "This is my beloved Son in Whom I am well pleased," John knew that this Lord Jesus was the Son of God. John had already professed his faith in Him because he could see that he had need to be baptized of Christ. Later, John was willing to deny himself utterly for the Lord Jesus Christ, for when men came to him and said, "Rabbi, He whom thou baptized beyond Jordan now baptizeth and all men go to Him," he said, "Did I not say unto you that a man can receive nothing unless he be given it from above? . . . I am not the Christ but I am sent before Him . . . He must increase but I must decrease." Here John revealed his willingness to set aside himself to exalt the Lord Jesus Christ, though it would mean his death, though it would mean the end of his ministry, the loss of his great audience, he was willing to do all for the Lord Jesus Christ. Finally, when he was apprehended and put in prison because of his courage, and the doubt began to enter into his soul, he sent two of his disciples unto the Lord Jesus to ask, "Art Thou He who should come, or look we for another?" In that sentence we can behold all of the sorrow, the loneliness, the heartache, the disappointment, the disillusionment, and the doubt of John's soul, for his revelation was imperfect. He knew not the kind of kingdom that the Lord Jesus was to establish, and when he did not see an earthly kingdom set up and himself liberated from prison, he began to doubt. The response the Lord Jesus gave to John is one that ought to reassure us all as to the nature of Christ's kingdom. He said, "Go and show John those things which ye do hear and see: the blind receive their sight, and the lame walk, the lepers are cleansed, and the deaf hear, the dead are raised up, and the poor have the gospel preached unto them, and blessed is he, whosoever shall not be offended in Me." Whatever faith John had at his death must have been reassured and strengthened by this statement of Christ.

John's greatness was also revealed in the powerful influence he exercised. First, that influence was revealed on Herod. Later, when Christ was teaching and was performing miracles and the multitudes assembled to Him, Herod said, "It is John the Baptist who has risen from the dead." Herod had beheaded John but believed that death could not hold him. His influence was also exerted on Jesus, for Jesus said concerning John, "What went ye forth into the wilderness for to see? A reed shaken with the wind? But what went ye out for to see? A man clothed in soft raiment? Behold, they that wear soft raiment are in king's houses. But what went ye forth for to see? A prophet? Yea, I say unto you, and more than a prophet, for this is he of whom it is written. Behold, I send My messenger before My face which shall prepare My way before thee. Verily I say unto you, among them that are born of women, there hath not arisen a greater than John the Baptist." Jesus forever placed John upon that pinnacle of greatness to which none other could ever come. Moreover, the people acknowledged John also as great, for when the Lord Jesus was in controversy with the Pharisees, He put the question to them, "The baptism of John, whence was it, from heaven or of men?" and they could not answer Him, because if they said, "From heaven," then their guilt would have been evident in not accepting him, and if they said "From men," they feared the people, because all the people accepted John as a great prophet. Here then we have Elisabeth living again in her son John, in great influence over the people, in great faith, and in great works before men.

III. ELISABETH AND JESUS

We have just quoted the words of Jesus in which He said, "Among all them that are born of women, there hath not arisen a greater than John the Baptist." Here we have the emphasis of Christ upon the part of woman in John's greatness. The Lord acknowledged that Elisabeth was partly responsible for the greatness of this son John, just as any mother is responsible for the greatness of her own son, but the Lord Jesus did not stop here. He said, "Notwithstanding he that is least in the kingdom of heaven is greater than he." In this we receive a teaching applicable to every mother who brings a son into the world.

The question arises: What then has the least believer now that John the Baptist did not have? The difference lies in the difference between the age of the law and that of grace, which were separated by the cross of Christ. The best that John or any of his age or any of those who preceded him could do was to hope for the promises of God. All believers, including Abraham, David, Solomon, Hezekiah, and Josiah, and the prophets, awaited Christ's coming and looked diligently into the promises to understand what manner of salvation this was that God had foretold, and yet they could not fully understand. The saints of old, including John the Baptist, were resting upon the promises. They could not say, blessed as they were, "My sins are blotted out. My iniquities are all gone." Before the death and resurrection of Christ, they could only look forward and say, "It shall be blessed indeed." They could be sure that it was God's intention, but they did not know it as an accomplished fact. They still had to come to God through the sacrifices of the priesthood, through the mediatorship of others. They could not come to Him directly as priests themselves into the presence of those things that were typified by the tabernacle and the law and the sacrifice. John was able to announce the kingdom is at hand, but John could not enter that kingdom. In John's day, the greatest in the sight of God could not enjoy the privileges of the least who were in the kingdom of God.

The kingdom means that reconciliation has been accomplished and that believers are in Christ, that they are born again, forgiven of their sin, justified in the presence of God, and accepted as righteous in His sight. Believers today are priests unto God. An inestimable value was set by God upon the death of Christ upon the cross, and because of that death He can accept sinful men in the beloved as His sons and as righteous in His sight. Now, because everything is done, God can invite souls not to forget their sin, not to turn away their eyes from them, but looking at them fairly and fully before the cross of Christ, He calls upon them to say, "The blood of Jesus Christ, His Son, cleanseth us from all sin." Knowing this, the priesthood today is not only superfluous but it is evil, for it separates the soul from God. Every believer is a priest now. It is the believer's God-given privilege to draw near to the holiest of all, with sin judged and his iniquities purged away, so that he may be thoroughly happy in the presence of God while he is still on earth.

This is not a promise, but it is a fact. The difference between a promise and an experience is the difference of being in prison with the promise that you will be brought out and the fact of your liberty when you are brought out. The difference is the difference between being in prison and having liberty. Thus the difference between John and the believer is the difference between having sin upon one, knowing that it will be forgiven, and the knowledge of having one's sin taken away through the cross of Christ.

The Woman Whose Son Was Greatest Of Men 77

The kingdom, then, means that one has complete assurance that because of the death of Christ, he is free from all sin. He is able to take his place in the sight of God exactly where Christ is. God gives us Christ's own standing in His sight. Through the ministry of the Holy Ghost, Who is now in the believer, the child of God is able to draw near unto the Father in the name of Christ, clothed in the nature of Christ, holding Christ's own standing before God, and thus able to ask God in the name of Christ for those things that are for the glory of Christ. This privilege is far beyond anything that could ever have been had or understood under the law. Thus, though John was the greatest of all in the Old Testament dispensation, the greatest of all outside the kingdom of God, the least Christian, the least believer, mediated by the death of Christ in his relationship with God, is greater than John the Baptist.

Whenever, then, a child is brought into the kingdom of God, both that child and he who brings him into the kingdom take a place greater than Elisabeth's and John the Baptist's. Elisabeth's son was the greatest of men, but the son of any spiritual believer, in faith may be greater than he. What a privilege then it is to be a mother in Israel of spiritual children, born through the travail of soul in prayer, born into the kingdom of God. The privileges of the kingdom of God are available for all now. We do not have to say, "Repent," as did John, "for the kingdom of God is at hand." We may say, "Repent and believe for the kingdom of God is here. The kingdom of God is yours for the taking. You should cry unto God that you might be acceptable unto Him as a child of the kingdom." And just as the dispensation that John announced came, so also that dispensation will come to its end, and with the end of this dispensation of grace, we shall have the end of the opportunity of being one of the world's greatest people, greater than Abraham, Isaac, Jacob, David, or John the Baptist, for surely the destiny of the church, according to the Scripture, will be higher and greater than that of any of the saved in all of the ages of the world's history.

Hence we hold out the promise to any man today that, though John the Baptist was great in character and in courage and in career, you may be greater than John in character because you are redeemed, in privilege, because of your standing in Christ, and in destiny because you will belong to the bride of Christ. The way to seal these privileges is to come to God by repentance, by faith, by trust in the Savior now, that you may be sealed through the gift of the Holy Ghost. Remember, "among those born of women there hath not arisen a greater than John the Baptist; notwithstanding the least in the kingdom of God is greater than he."

VI

THE WOMAN WHO TURNED TEMPTRESS

The woman whom thou gavest to be with me, she gave me of the tree, and I did eat.

THE environment for the event that forms the basis of our discussion was absolutely perfect. It was the garden that God planted in Eden for the habitation of the first man whom He had created. What a glorious garden that was! In it was everything that was good; every kind of flower that was beautiful to the eye, every tree upon which man loves to look, every shrub to break the abruptness of the contrast between the trees and the flowers, every herb, every vine, every moss, every lichen that would contribute to the beauty of the place. Trees, shrubs, and plants we would travel far to see were there in great profusion and yet in order and in loveliness. Truly it was a garden, not a jungle. There was no thorn there, or brier or thistle or weed. The profuse beauty, the perfumed odors, the panorama of colors, all were those of valuable plants rather than hurtful.

In this garden there was no death. All animals from the least to the greatest were there, named by the first man and manifesting the beauty of their strength and body, but they were not beasts of prey. There was no animal that lived upon the flesh of another animal. They lived together in harmony. All were vegetarian, and to them was given such a range of food that they would never desire the flesh of another animal. Hence in that garden there was no pain. There was no disease. There was no hurt. There was no sorrow; all of which contributes toward death. Instead there was nothing but happiness, pleasure, and delight for all creatures living in this pristine harmony and glory. There was not even a rain cloud in the sky, for the Lord did not cause it to rain upon the earth but watered it by means of a mist that came up from the earth. There were mountains, rivers, lakes, and seas, but there was no den of snakes to mar the security of the forest and no man-eating sharks in the bays or seas. In fact, the Garden of Eden was perfect. It was all that the wisdom of an infinite God could make it. How this thought must stimulate a lover of nature, who delights over a scene of tranquility in the hills and the lakes, whose soul is enraptured over the beauty of an ancient oak or fir and who even loves the mica-flaked rocks of the mountains! What an experience it must have been to have lived in the Garden of Eden!

This garden was only possible after the six days of creation, which occurred under the instrumentality of an infinite and omnipotent God. The Bible accurately pictures the wonders of those six days. The more we read this narrative, the more we realize that there is nothing in it that is contrary in any respect to the findings of science. We read that God created the heavens and the earth and then we read the first hint of a pristine judgment that came upon the world in connection with some other creation than that of man. It says that the earth was without form and void. Later these very words are used by Jeremiah and Isaiah as referring to some judgment that occurred upon the earth in connection with the fall of Satan and his angels from heaven. In the interval between this and the beginning of the six days of God's creation, we have room for all the periods of geologic time. In this judgment, great animals that once roamed the earth were turned into fossils. Mountains were heaved up from the deep, and deposits of oil, radium, and helium were made in the earth. There is no reason to believe that in this earthly judgment, the seeds of life were not retained in the earth. There is no reason to believe that the sun was not already created, although

The Woman Who Turned Temptress 81

obscured in darkness, so that when the Lord began to remodel the earth, He first was able to bring forth the light of the sun that had been shrouded in the darkness of mists. Then the Lord created the airy and gaseous heavens, beyond which is darkness and without which there could be no life upon the earth. In the third period of remodeling the world, the Lord brought the land together out of the waters and caused the land to bring forth grass, herbs, fruit-trees, and plant life, yielding seed after its kind. Then the Lord commanded that the lights of the firmament appear, and He set them as signs and for seasons and days and years to rule over the changes upon the earth. Then on the fifth day, we read that the Lord again exercised the power of creation and created the living things in the waters of the earth and also the fowl of the heavens. Following this, He caused the earth to bring forth many kinds of animals, each after his own kind, and lastly exercised again the power of creation and made man in His own image in order that he should have dominion over the fish of the sea, the fowl of the air, and the cattle of the earth. It was for this crowning creature of God's making that He planted a garden in Eden. This man was formed of the dust of the ground, breathed into by the breath of life, and became a living soul in the image of God.

Regardless of the way in which God developed the various species that were found in the garden, or the time it took Him to do so in His own good pleasure, we have in that garden, not a jungle of the survival of the fittest, but a paradise of harmony and of blessing. We ought to note that it was in this place that the fall occurred for the human race. It was not in a back alley of some slum or during a war scene upon earth, or in the midst of a great depression, but it was in the midst of peace and plenty and prosperity and harmony. This fact once and for all refutes what is called "The Social Gospel," in which we are told that man's nature can be changed by his environment or by his education. We are very happy to grant a large place to environment and to education in the influences that have been brought to bear upon the actions of men, but we do not believe that these factors can make man good. It is the old story of the pig in the parlor. His surroundings do not change his nature. If man chose evil when he was perfect in his nature and perfect in his surroundings, how much easier is it for man to choose evil in the kind of surroundings with a nature he has today? With all that environment can do for a person, it is not enough. It was not enough to preserve man from sin in the beginning. It was in this paradise of God that sin occurred.

I. THE STATE OF WOMAN BEFORE THE TEMPTATION

If man generically speaking was the highest in God's series of creations because he was the last, then woman takes a higher place than man as the acme of creation because within the species of man she followed the male. There were three steps in creation. Three times the word "bara," to create, is used in the Bible. The first is when it says, "In the beginning God created the heavens and the earth." The second concerns life when it says, "And God created every living creature that moveth." And the third is in reference to man, when it says, "So God created man in his own image." At these three places, the evolutionists are forever frustrated because they cannot produce any theory that can account for the beginning of the world. *Ex nihilo nihil est.* Either the universe must be eternal or else God created it. There is no other alternative. Second, the evolutionists are never able to present any evidence of spontaneous generation of life. There must have been a beginning to the process of life. Third, although the evolutionist may be able to reconstruct a primitive man from a tooth or a jaw-bone or from some other part of the body, he has utterly no proof that there ever was a transition from animal life to human life, wherein the mind and soul of

The Woman Who Turned Temptress 83

man differentiate him from the beast. At these three stages, the Bible says that God created, and human experience vindicates that teaching.

Between these stages there is great room for development. We have no means to know how long the days were that are spoken of in the Book of Genesis. They may have been long eras of time, and it may have been the good pleasure of God to develop the various species in ways according to His will. There is room for evolution in one's thinking when it is taken to mean development within these limitations under the power of God, but not in any other way. At the end of this great process, as the final act of Deity before He entered into His Sabbath rest, there came the creation of woman. She was not only the last, but she was the best. She was absolutely perfect. Some woman in body may resemble a Venus de Milo and appear to be perfect. Another woman may have a very developed mind, with the keenest of mental power. Yet another may be of a spirit that seems to be beyond the reach of mortal man, and yet these qualities are never combined in one person. There is always some limitation. Imagine the finest woman who ever lived, in body, mind, and spirit, or choose any three and combine them in one, and still we have a creature who is unequal to the first woman whom God created.

The story of the creation of woman is a very suggestive one in relationship to her position as helpmeet for man. Although man had a perfect place in which to live, every imaginable kind of beast and bird and creature with which to play or to work, or which he might dominate, he nevertheless was alone. There was a wide gulf that separated man from every creature of the world. Frederick the Great was able to say, "The more I see of people, the more I like my dog," but that is not true of humanity in general. It cannot be true. Man for awhile may be satisfied with horses and dogs and birds, but that is impossible permanently. Man found himself alone, and God said, "It is not good that man should be alone. I will make him an helpmeet for him." Hence, the Lord made woman. Ancient commentators were accustomed to refer to the way in which the Scripture says God created woman in order to show her station in relationship to man. God did not take woman from man's head, as Hera is supposed to have sprung full grown from the head of Jove, lest man worship her. Neither did he take her from his feet, lest he use her as a slave: but God took her from one of his ribs, near the heart, in order that He might love her and recognize her as his equal, protecting her with the power of his arm. The Lord never intended woman to be inferior to man, and as the processes of redemption are fulfilled, woman will again be placed on an equal with man in every sense of the word. This, in fact, is one of the fruits of Calvary, which is gradually being wrought out in the world in our dispensation.

The relation between man and woman was to be that of monogamous marriage. In response to His disciples' question about divorce, the Lord Jesus referred to this event by saying, "Have ye not read that He which made them at the beginning, made them male and female, and said, for this cause shall a man leave father and mother and shall cleave to his wife: and they twain shall be one flesh? Wherefore they are no more twain, but one flesh. What therefore God hath joined together, let not man put asunder." With the exception of the last sentence, which Christ Himself added, this quotation is taken from the Book of Genesis. Any departure from this high standard was, according to Christ, permitted of God only because of the hardness of men's hearts, and from the beginning it was not so, for God intended man and woman to live in a monogamous relationship of marriage.

We may assume that the first man and woman were extremely happy together. It would be easy to use one's imagination and to reconstruct the scenes of fellowship and

The Woman Who Turned Temptress

of love they had in the garden, walking in the cool of the day or in the early morn. Theirs must have been a bliss as unclouded as that which will be ours in heaven, with perfect understanding, with perfect love that knew no ending, and with perfect balance in their natures, made one for the other. Theirs was the ideal marriage, the ideal love, and the ideal happiness.

Added to all this was the fact that God walked with Adam and Eve in the garden. After their fall, we read that they heard the voice of the Lord God walking in the garden in the cool of the day, and the implication is that it was the habit of the Lord to manifest Himself unto that first couple. The Lord made man for His own fellowship and enjoyment. Then we may be sure that He revealed His affection to them in the garden in fellowship. Here might truly be said:

He walks with Me and He talks with me,
And He tells me I am His own.
The joy we share as we tarry there,
None other has ever known.

There is no fellowship like the fellowship with God. To walk with God is the highest privilege given to man upon earth. Adam enjoyed the undimmed fellowship of the Creator.

In the midst of this fellowship, the Lord gave the first man and first woman a commandment. He said, "Of every tree of the garden thou mayest freely eat, but of the tree of the knowledge of good and evil, thou shalt not eat of it, for in the day that thou eatest thereof thou shalt surely die." We read that the tree of life was also in the center of the garden, and there was no command that man should not eat of it. It is possible that God permitted this in order to see whether man would eat first of the tree of life, which would truly make him like unto God, or whether he would eat first of the tree of the knowledge of good and evil, which was forbidden. This commandment of God is what is known as the covenant of works. It is the requirement that man shall live by doing. In the day that he violates the commandment of God, he will surely die. The requirement of perfect obedience of the divine will in order to have eternal life or to be as God in nature is still a requirement of God for man. Because this perfect obedience is the requirement of God, it excludes, then, all men from salvation by works, for no man, from Adam until now, with the exception of the Lord Jesus Christ, has perfectly done the will of God during a period of trial. It was during this probation, when man and woman were in a state of perfection, that the temptation came.

II. The Woman as Temptress

The fact that the woman became the temptress assumes that she had fallen. In order to be the instrument of evil, woman first had to subject herself to evil. Hence we turn our attention to the temptation of the woman by the serpent. The Scripture clearly says that the devil assumed the form of a serpent. This statement is not included in the story of Eve and Adam, but it is placed in the narrative in later Scripture. Here again we have a mere suggestion of what must have happened back before the foundation of the world, as we know it today, when the fall of Satan from being Lucifer caused him to contend against God's creation wherever he could. That controversy with God now manifested itself in the sphere of humanity.

The methods used by Satan on Eve are the methods by which we may detect his presence and activity in the world today. They have not changed. His temptation of the woman is almost identical with his temptation of the Lord Jesus. He appealed to them both through the lust of the eyes, the love of the world, and the pride of life. First, Satan questioned the Word of God as to its source. He said, "Hath God said?" He suggested that the commandment they received was not from God at all. After the

The Woman Who Turned Temptress

woman repeated the commandment to him as the Lord had given it to them, for she knew it well, he then questioned its truth. He said, "Ye shall not surely die," and then, finally, he questioned its justice, or the motive of God in doing it. He said, "For God doth know that in the day that ye eat thereof then your eyes shall be opened and ye shall be as God knowing good and evil." Whether we see the activity of Satan with this first woman, or with Job, or again with the Lord Jesus Christ, it is ever the same. He thought that when Christ saw the kingdoms of the world, He would fall down and worship him, or when He heard a misquotation of the Word of God, that He would act upon it in presumption, or that He would use His power for His own end. Where he did not succeed with the second Adam, he succeeded with the first human pair. It says, "When the woman saw that the tree was good for food, and that it was pleasant to the eye, and a tree to be desired to make one wise, she took of the fruit thereof and did eat." Here we see that she first considered. She saw that it was pleasant to the eye. Then she desired it because it was good for food, and also because it was to make one wise, and though she knew the contrary command of God, she acted upon this out of her aroused desire. Once the woman had sinned, evil was no longer without, being suggested through a serpent, or a third party, but now it was within the woman, and hereinafter she became the temptress. Satan was now able to leave his work to her. We do not read that he appeared to or conversed with man. He abandoned his cause now to the woman. She became the temptress.

The description of the fall of man is very simple. It says, "The woman also gave unto her husband with her and he did eat." Man rationally, intentionally, and voluntarily entered into sin. One may imagine, if he will, the wearing of Eve upon Adam as the wife of Potiphar gradually bore her cause in upon Joseph until finally he fled from her presence, or as the daughter of Timnath wept upon Samson until he told her his riddle, or as Delilah even wept over Samson because he kept his secret from her, until he finally told her, and thus was brought low, or as any other woman has won her way with a man, and see how gradually Adam weakened until he gave in to the woman. Adam had weighed the consequences well. He knew what it meant. He had looked back to the time when he was alone and looked forward to a time when, if this woman was judged of God, he might be left alone again. So he made his choice deliberately. He chose the presence of this woman whom he loved, with sin, rather than to have holiness without her. Certainly much can be said about the affections of Adam in this case. Had, however, his decision been otherwise, we are persuaded to believe that the history of the human race might have been different. As it was, man and woman both sinned, and as the progenitors of the human race, the mother and the father of all living, they communicated to all men the guilt of this sin, as well as the propensity to further sin.

That there was guilt in the action of this woman and the subsequent action of the man is evident from the fact that now their eyes were opened and they knew that they were naked, and they sewed fig leaves together to cover their nakedness. No longer were they innocent. The half truth of Satan had been fulfilled. They were now as God. They knew the difference between right and wrong, but they also carried with them that terrible sense of guilt in the presence of God, for soon they heard God walking in the garden in the cool of the day, and they hid themselves from the presence of the Lord because of the sense of their guilt. The voice of God seeking out Adam in the cool of the day is a voice seeking out man throughout the world today, saying, "Where art thou?" and our excuses are just as flimsy. Adam said, "I heard Thy voice in the garden and I was afraid because I was naked, and I hid myself." The

The Woman Who Turned Temptress

Lord knew then that man had eaten of the forbidden tree. In the inquisition for guilt that followed, the primary responsibility was placed upon the serpent, who was the instrument of the devil, and the secondary responsibility upon the woman and upon man. The punishments for each were fitting. As to the serpent, there was to be enmity between it and the seed of the woman, and there came a physical change in the structure of the serpent itself. Though it is still unto this day a graceful creature, it must have been a beautiful one before the time of its curse. The punishment of the woman was that in sorrow she should bring forth children and her husband should rule over her all her days. To Adam, He said, "Cursed is the ground for thy sake. In sorrow shalt thou eat of it all the days of thy life. Thorns also, and thistles shall it bring forth to thee; and thou shalt eat the herb of the field. In the sweat of thy face shalt thou eat bread, till thou return unto the ground." The fulfillment of these curses is evident in every realm of life today. It is said that wherever there is virgin soil, as on an island where man has never set foot, there are no thorns or thistles and that they only come after the advent of man. The labor of man and of woman is a daily experience, whereas the serpent is an object of human antipathy.

III. THE WOMAN AS THE MEANS OF VICTORY OVER TEMPTATION

In the midst of the curse upon the woman, however, there came a promise. God said, "Between thy seed and her seed, I will put enmity. It shall bruise thy head and thou shalt bruise his heel." The chain of references that begins here includes the promises and the prophecies concerning Christ that were fulfilled in His birth and His works at His first advent. Eve understood and believed this promise, which was later enlarged for her descendants, enlarged again to Abraham, and continually amplified down to the very time of the Lord Jesus Christ. In His death upon the cross, Satan bruised His heel, but there also He bruised the head of Satan. The Lord Jesus said as He went to the cross, "Now is the prince of this world cast out." His power was broken upon Calvary. Christ was the Lamb of God Who taketh away the sin of the world, and it was as such that Eve saw Him in this very first promise given to her in the Garden of Eden at the time of her sin. Thus it was that the seed of the woman was ultimately to become the means of victory over temptation, over sin, and over death. We must never forget that Christ came into the world born of a woman.

The belief in these promises by Eve is given a clear evidence in the birth of her firstborn son. The fourth chapter of Genesis, the first verse, says, "Eve conceived and bare Cain and said, I have gotten a man from the Lord." In the original Hebrew, the phrase "from the" is omitted. Eve said, "I have gotten a man, the very Lord." Eve thought that the promise of a Messiah or a Savior born of a woman, Who was to be God and able to overcome Satan, was fulfilled in her firstborn son, who became Cain. In this she was mistaken, just as many of the godly and pious women of Israel were mistaken in their hope that the children born of them should be the Messiah, until the annunciation was made to Mary in Nazareth of Galilee, but Eve had faith and because of this faith in the coming Redeemer, she was saved. It was a faith such as hers that gave salvation unto Sarah and Rachel, to Abraham, to David, to Jacob, to Hezekiah, to the long line of Old Testament saints. It is the belief in this promise that has now been fulfilled which gives salvation to any man or any woman today. In the fulness of time, born under the law, made of a woman, came He Who was to redeem us from the curse of the law, from the curse of sin, and from the power of temptation. He Who knew no sin was made subject unto death for us that He might deliver us from the power of death, even from the devil, that old serpent.

Woman has also been the means of victory over temptation for man because of her obedience. Because woman has known what Christ has done for her and what He will do for her, woman has led man in all things pertaining to worship of the Lord Jesus Christ. Because of what God has done for her, she has been full of gratitude and of love and adoration for Him and has taken the leadership in the work of the church throughout history. Thus it is we look to woman today as a mediator of blessing and victory for men in matters of faith.

When God finished conversing with man, we read that "The Lord God made coats of skins and clothed them." These skins were undoubtedly a divinely intended type of Christ, Who was made unto us righteousness, for the righteousness of Christ is the garment with which sinners are clothed and made fit for the presence of God. It is interesting to note that these were the skins of animals, which meant that God slew the first animal in order that there might be a blood sacrifice for the salvation of man and the covering of his sins. God was able to overlook the sins that were past because of Him Who was to come, even Christ, Who made a propitiation for our sins through the shedding of His blood. It was for this reason that Abel's sacrifice of a lamb of the flock was acceptable before God and Cain's was not. God had undoubtedly taught the first man and woman that without the shedding of blood there was no remission of sin. With sin came suffering and death. There had to be a substitute for man for which God chose the lamb as typical of the Lamb of God Who would take away the sin of the world.

Though the eternal punishment of their sin was undoubtedly forgiven, the temporal punishment was not remitted. Lest man, now in his mortal state and sinful condition, eat of the tree of life and live forever without redemption, the Lord drove man out of the Garden of Eden to till the cursed ground from whence he was taken, and He set, as the

Scripture says, Cherubim, and the flaming sword that turned every way, to keep the way of the tree of life. With hope for eternity, hope for life in the presence of God, which he had once known, with a memory from which he could never escape, Adam now went forth to endure the trials and sufferings of life until death should overtake him, for through the influence of woman, he was visited with death, and yet through the influence of that same woman and her glorious Son, even the Lord Jesus Christ, he will be visited with life through the resurrection. Though through the influence of women as temptress the human race has eaten of the tree of the knowledge of good and evil, yet through woman also it will eat of the tree of life and live forever.

VII
THE WOMAN WHO WAS BETRAYED

And David sent and inquired after this woman and one said, Is not this Bath-sheba, the daughter of Eliam, the wife of Uriah the Hittite?

THE meaning of "betrayal" is customarily associated with the betrayal of a woman by a man through falseness, but this is not the only means of betrayal. One, however, would naturally associate such with the title of this sermon. Evidently there was much of this falseness of man to woman in the lawless times represented by certain sections of the Bible. As the human race degenerated, more and more woman was treated lightly and as a plaything of man, to be violated when he pleased. These heathen practices sometimes affected Israel and seeped into the national life of the people of God. Under the advice of Balaam in the matter of Beth Peor, the Israelites were led into great sin through this practice, but the Hebrew laws expressly forbade it, and they correctly divided responsibility between the man and the woman so that through the respective punishments this practice should be utterly wiped out from the commonwealth of the people of God. Such sin was called "folly in Israel."

There were, however, numerous examples of this folly. Once Dinah, the daughter of Jacob, went to visit the daughters of the land in Shechem, where the Israelites were sojourning in their wanderings. There she was found by a prince of the land, the son of Hamor, and was betrayed by him. The wrong was so keenly felt by the sons of Jacob that they, in turn, through trickery, were enabled to avenge themselves upon the whole of the city and, unreasonably, they slew all the males in the city, an act strongly condemned by Jacob himself. Another incident is that of Amnon and Tamar. Tamar was the beautiful sister of Absalom, the favorite son of David. Her half-brother, Amnon, loved her and, through the advice of a child of Belial, was able to betray her. Again it was called "folly in Israel," and this time it was punished with death. Absalom invited his brother Amnon and the other brothers of the kingly family to a feast and during the feast Amnon was slain; everyone knew that it was because he had wronged Absalom's sister. Yet as we read the history of the people of Israel over a period of sixteen hundred years, we are amazed that there are so remarkably few incidents of this in the narrative. Wherever they appear, it is with strong condemnation from the Hebrew law.

The last great case was that of David and Bath-sheba. It becomes the outstanding example in the Bible, one filled with many lessons for those who will study it. God certainly did not put this in the Bible in order that it might be suppressed in our thinking and teaching. However, had it not appeared in the Bible, no minister would ever presume to select it out of any other type of literature in order to make it a topic of a sermon, for it contains dreadful sins. Alexander Whyte says that it is in the Bible in order that we might realize that even the heroes of the faith are men of like passions as we are, to show us that the saints were not so far above us but we, in turn, can rise to their level.

Not in their brightness, but their earthly stains,
Are the true scenes vouchsafed to earthly eyes,
And saints are lowered that the world may rise.

Under the word "betrayal" there is also the thought that immediately comes to one of the betrayal of one's country or of one's friends. Especially is this so at the Passion season of Christ, when we are thinking of the great drama centered around His person and the betrayal that concerned

The Woman Who Was Betrayed 95

Him. Certainly the act of Judas of selling his Lord and Master to the Jews in order that they might accuse Him and turn Him over to the Romans to be put to death is the acme of faithlessness we consider under the word "betrayal." Truly Jesus "was wounded in the house of His friends." He even called Judas "friend" in the Garden when he kissed Him in order to designate Him as the One whom the soldiers were to apprehend. Many men through history have taken their places with Judas in our estimation. There is, for one, Benedict Arnold, who for a miserable sum and a promise of station in the British life, sold the secrets of his country to an enemy. Though the early exploits of Arnold were of great heroism and patriotism, nevertheless this stain upon his character forever brands him as an outcast in the thinking of true Americans. Following him, there was Aaron Burr, who was accused of conceiving a means of treason by which a large section of the United States would fall to a foreign country over which he, in turn, ultimately might preside. These were acts of betrayal large enough to be noted by all men; but there are many acts of betrayal that are accomplished daily and of denials both to Christ and to our friends that should brand many men as traitors and as faithless. These do not become generally known.

One of the commonest acts of betrayal in life is that of a woman by a woman. Well did Paul say that the younger women should marry and bear children and guide the house and give none occasion to the adversary to speak reproachfully, for he said he had learned that some of them wandered about from house to house and were not only idle but tattlers also, and busybodies, speaking things which they ought not. He went even farther and said that no man should ever be elected a deacon whose wife was given to slander. Some of the most terrible wounds that are ever given to men and women are given in the house of their friends through the use of the tongue. Why women in particular are subject to petty ambitions, jealousies, and envies of life is hard to know, but experience has certainly vindicated the truth of the teaching of the Apostle Paul. Sometimes even professing Christians will allow these petty things to assume mountainous size and, though they act as friends to the faces of their women acquaintances, they do the most dastardly lying through innuendo, gossip, and slander behind their backs. This seems to be one of the devil's favorite pastimes, but all women who are tempted to engage in such sin or who have already engaged in it should be warned that justice will avenge them as surely as it avenged the action of Judas or of Benedict Arnold or of David or of anyone else guilty of betrayal. The reaping begins immediately with the act in lowering the character of the gossiper or the slanderer. The law, "whatsoever you sow you will also reap," immediately comes into operation.

I. The Woman Who Was Betrayed

It has been the habit when thinking of Bath-sheba to think of the sinfulness of David in betraying her, and no one would ever excuse David for his actions in this case. His soul must have been as dark as night and his action as culpable as anything that Satan ever did, but in spite of it, David was not the only one who sinned. It is this fact that has often been overlooked. We learn sufficient about Bath-sheba from the story to justify us in passing a judgment upon her conduct, for certainly she was an accomplice of David in this sin.

Bath-sheba's responsibility lay in three things. First, she was immodest, or David would never have been led to the sin. Second, she submitted to David's desire without any protest. Third, she concealed the event from her own husband, Uriah. Whenever a woman is deliberately immodest, she brings upon herself the judgment of salacious reckless-

The Woman Who Was Betrayed 97

ness. In order to understand this in the case of Bath-sheba, one must know a bit about the construction of houses in Jerusalem in that ancient day. There the roofs were all flat and were commonly used as a place of refreshment in the cool evening air for the inhabitants of the city. Since the houses were closely joined one to another, any commanding eminence could overlook the roofs of other houses. Evidently David's palace was hard by the home of Uriah and overlooked its roof. Certainly all this was known to Bath-sheba, and yet she mounted to the roof of her house at eventide and, with a possibility that she would be seen by someone from the roof of an adjoining house, she publicly exposed herself. Granting that this was mere immodesty and not a deliberate act upon her part, we still hold that Bath-sheba was responsible for a definite part in the sin of David, for it was at that moment that David was walking upon the roof of the palace and he beheld her and had awakened in him the temptation to which he succumbed.

Next we read that when David sent messengers to bring Bath-sheba to the palace, she came. Moreover, we have recorded no conversation, no remonstrance, merely a rapid passing over of the events that became the cause of his later crime. Yet when we turn back to a heathen queen such as Vashti, in the time of Ahasuerus, we are told that when she was commanded to be immodest and to present herself before the banquet of the king that she refused even at the cost of her throne. Ahasuerus was of a greater power as an Oriental monarch than even David, for David was compelled to act according to law. Having heard no outcry, having no record of any resistance or any remonstrance on the part of Bath-sheba, we may assume that she submitted voluntarily to the act and thus she could not be without guilt.

Third, when Bath-sheba's husband, Uriah, was called home from the battle front by David and slept by the door of David's house, Bath-sheba sent him no word nor did she even communicate with him personally to tell him what had happened, to denounce the king, and to confess with tearful eyes and with a grieved soul of the shame that had been wrought upon her. It seems that she even condescended to the plan of David of disposing of her husband in order that she might be added to the harem of the king. A careful reading of this narrative, which in part lays the great blame upon David, and rightly so, will leave one with the impression that Bath-sheba certainly was not without her sin as an accomplice in this act.

For this reason, Bath-sheba was not without her suffering. After Uriah was dead and she had been married to the king and the child who was conceived in sin was born, God struck the child and it was very sick. David was so moved by the suffering of Bath-sheba and by his own love for the child that he fasted and wept and prayed and lay upon the earth seven days without eating or drinking in order to gain the mercy of God for the child. If this is a description of what David did, what must have been happening in the case of Bath-sheba? Undoubtedly in this experience she recognized the hand of God chastening her for her part in the sin. We may well imagine the grief of her soul, the tears that flowed, the prayers she uttered, the contrition she manifested, and then the sorrow in the death of the child. The Lord was to punish David still farther, but the primary punishment of the beautiful woman, Bath-sheba, came to her in connection with the loss of this little one, who had already entwined its fingers around her heart.

Many years later an event occurred in the life of David ––just before his death—that tells us David made compensation and restitution to Bath-sheba for the wrong he had done. He may have done it in the days of her suffering because of the loss of the child. David was now an old man and Adonijah, his son, had declared that he was king. Then Nathan sent Bath-sheba to converse with the king about Solomon, her son, and she said, "My lord, thou swearest by the Lord thy God unto thine handmaid, saying, assuredly Solomon thy son shall reign after me, and he shall sit upon my throne." Then the king answered Bath-sheba with an oath, saying, "As the Lord liveth, that hath redeemed my soul out of all distress, even as I sware unto thee by the Lord God of Israel, saying, assuredly Solomon thy son shall reign after me, and he shall sit upon my throne in my stead; even so will I certainly do this day." Sometime in this early relationship, when under contrition, sorrow, remorse, and even repentance this couple suffered, David with an oath swore unto God that he would make this compensation to Bath-sheba. It had been so long past that he had almost forgotten it, but undoubtedly it was done in order to lessen her suffering. However we look upon Bath-sheba, whether as one who was innocent or guilty, she suffered severely from this wrong.

II. The Man Who Betrayed Her

The Bible is exceedingly candid in revealing the sins of the heroes of the faith. In any other book but the Bible, where the biography of this man was being presented, this would have been suppressed, but the Bible tells this incident in its greatest detail. Here was a man called a man after God's own heart and yet one who fell terribly and sinned grievously in the sight of God. Surely this, instead of being an evidence against the Bible as the Word of God, is an example of its inspiration, for by means of this event the divine mercy and judgment were revealed and demonstrated in behalf of man. The fact that God knows everything and suppresses nothing and has said that everything will be made known, even that which is hidden here on earth, ought to bring stark fear to the hearts of some people for taking comfort in covering the sins in which they have indulged. There is only one way to be safe after you have sinned, namely, to confess that sin and openly to acknowledge it in the sight of God and of those whom you have wronged in order that it may forever be put away from you.

There were definite steps in David's fall, which may be of value to us in warning and teaching. His temptation came to him at a time when kings went forth to battle. The Bible implies that David should have been at the head of his armies in the siege of Rabbah instead of languishing at ease in his palace in Jerusalem. A long process of inner corruption must have already taken place in David to weaken him and make him ready for such a fall, and that process is shown by the fact that he was taking his ease when Israel dwelt in tents. Uriah emphasized this when David urged him to go to his home and sent a mess of meat after him that he might enjoy himself. Said he, "The ark, and Israel, and Judah, abide in tents; and my lord Joab, and the servants of my lord, are encamped in the open fields; shall I then go into mine house, to eat and to drink . . . as thy soul liveth, I will not do this thing." Uriah had the attitude David should have had. Next, when David saw the object of temptation, instead of immediately putting it from his mind, he toyed with it as a thought until he was consumed with desire and driven to action. However, he then excused himself; he had a right as an absolute monarch to do this thing; since he had lived so close to God during his whole life he could now afford one indulgence. He, nevertheless, knew that it was contrary to the will of God, Who had established him upon his throne, and he deliberately sinned. Just one such sin is able to spoil the entire life of a saint of God and bring him low. In one instant, one can undo the work of a lifetime. By one fall, the influence we exercised over many may be completely ruined.

The resulting sin was of so shocking a character that we cannot dwell upon it. It is horrible and repulsive and it ought not even to be associated with the name of a man after God's own heart. It was an act of ignominious adultery of the plainest kind. Secondly, it included the act of intoxicating his friend in an effort to conceal his own guilt. Third, when this artifice failed, it included the deliberate murder of an innocent and faithful officer of his army. It was the concealing of his sin even more than the sin itself which, according to the Scripture, displeased the Lord.

During the period that followed David's condition was anything but pleasant. It lasted approximately twelve months from the time of his sin until the time of the revelation of that sin. This has been called by Bishop Butler a time of self-deceit in the life of David. It cannot be overlooked that it was after a twelvemonth of deceit, internal hypocrisy, and self-forgiving silence on David's part that Nathan was sent to David with the message of divine indignation. "How a man like David could have lived all that time soaked to the eyes in adultery and murder and not go mad is simply inconceivable." Bishop Butler goes on to show how that this self-deception is the heart of the sin of each of us. We condone ourselves when we judge others. This may be the reason that David was so intensely and unusually cruel in his treatment of the people of Rabbah when they were conquered by the armies of Israel. However we interpret the verse that describes this, it still is a cruel treatment. While we condone our own sins, we are often severe judges of others. Moreover, when Nathan came to David with his parable of an unjust, wealthy man who stole the lamb from the poor man, David's wrath flashed in righteous indignation. He was hypocritically showing himself to be a righteous judge of others while completely excusing himself.

The Scripture says that this sin of David gave occasion for the enemies of the Lord to blaspheme. There are many things in the narrative concerning Joab that would lead us to believe that he was a true believer. On the other hand, there are many things that lead us to believe that he was not. David commanded his son Solomon that after his death Joab should be judged for his sins he had done of murder of innocent men, and Joab was put to death. I suppose that when Joab learned of this particular sin of David, he then was able the more readily to excuse himself for the wrongs that he had done. Then there was Shimei, who cursed David and who was wicked in heart. There was Ziba, the servant of Mephibosheth, who had done wrong, and I suppose the kingdom was full of evil-doers, who now took comfort for the things that they had done that were wrong because the king had set them the standard and had excused himself for at least a year. This is something of an example of what sins of believers do in the church and to the world. Whenever someone who professes to be a leader in the church is guilty of a wicked violation of God's law and covers it up, though the world knows about it, he sets the example for others and helps them along the road to hell. Better is it by far that we should judge ourselves and cleanse ourselves from all iniquity than to set a stumbling-block in the way of someone else.

III. THE BETRAYER IN THE HANDS OF GOD

After it was evident that David was to excuse, to forgive, and to condone himself for the things that he had done by one argument or another, and that he would not be led to confession and repentance through his own self-judgment, God sent a messenger to him, the prophet Nathan. To be pointed at and to be told to his face that he was unclean and cruel and cowardly and guilty of blood was David's salvation. "To have someone injured enough and angry enough, or friendly and honest enough and kind enough to call you to your face false, or cruel, or envious, or malicious, or hard-hearted, or ignorant and narrow-minded and full of prejudice and party spirit, or meek to the great and harsh to the poor, or all that together, might be the beginning of your salvation." Such a person instead of being your enemy would be your greatest friend. The Scripture says, "Let the righteous smite me; it shall be a kindness: and let him reprove me; it shall be an excellent oil, which shall not break my head." Thus it was that Nathan came with his story saying, "There were two men in one city; the one rich, and the other poor. The rich man had exceeding many flocks and herds: but the poor man had nothing, save one little ewe lamb, which he had bought and nourished up: and it grew up together with him, and with his children; it did eat of his own meat, and drank of his own cup, and lay in his bosom, and was unto him as a daughter. And there came a traveler unto the rich man, and he spared to take of his own flock and of his own herd, to dress for the wayfaring man that was come unto him; but he took the poor man's lamb, and dressed it for the man that was come to him." To this picture of domestic happiness and beauty there came tragedy—stark, cruel, awful tragedy—and it struck David's sense of pity and of justice. In wrath, David cried, "As the Lord liveth, the man that hath done this thing shall surely die: and he shall restore the lamb fourfold, because he did this thing, and because he had no pity." Little did David know that the sword of God's justice and judgment was hanging within but a hairbreadth of his own head, but now it began to cut his conscience. Said Nathan, "Thou art the man. You were the king of Israel and possessed riches and comforts, palaces, servants, wives, slaves and concubines, and if that had been too little, I would have given thee such and such things. Wherefore, then, hast thou despised the commandment of the Lord to do evil in His sight? Thou hast killed Uriah the Hittite with the sword and taken his wife to be thy wife, and thou hast slain him with the sword of the children of Ammon." How much better it would have been for David had he allowed his own conscience to smite him first, to play the part of God and the part of Nathan the prophet! How much better for him had he confessed these things privately, before they were revealed publicly and he was made an object lesson for the Lord! Even so, it is better for us today to take our sins out and confess them openly and make restitution before that which is hidden is revealed in the justice of an infinite God. The wisdom and delicacy of Nathan in preaching this sermon to David is very beautiful. Often we thunder and we blunder and we fail to lead men to repentance, but before David even knew it, the sword of the Word of God lodged itself in his heart and rather than turn against his friend Nathan for preaching against him, he turned against himself and condemned himself in the eyes of God. Surely when Nathan made that speech to David, he was but a step from death, for an Oriental monarch could have confined him easily to the dungeon or commanded his death, but instead, David said, "I have sinned against the Lord."

David's repentance was immediate. As soon as he saw himself as God saw him, as a pitiless, selfish, and heartless monarch, as one who had everything and yet spared not another man's little, he cried out in self-loathing, aversion, and confession of his sin. This whole story is unlike the David, the noble, blessed David of the Old Testament, whom we love, whom we know. Deep in his heart he was not this way, and as soon as he saw himself as God now saw him, he was smitten in heart and repented. There were no excuses given by David now. There was no false repentance. There was no condoning of self. There was only a sense of transgression. Just as quickly as David repented, God forgave him, for Nathan said, "The Lord also hath put away thy sin; thou shalt not die. Howbeit . . ." Then he went on to tell of the punishment that would come upon David.

Because David had given the enemies of the Lord occasion to blaspheme by his act, therefore, the enemies of the Lord must see that David should suffer for the things that he had done, at the hands of a righteous God. The first punishment that should come upon him was that the sword would never depart from his house. What an awful prediction this was for a man whose throne God had promised to establish forever and ever! First, we see the sword as it flashes in the hands of Absalom, killing his brother Amnon for what he did to Tamar. Next we see the sword flashing in the hands of Joab as it pierced the heart of Absalom while he hung in the tree. Again we see the sword flashing as thousands rose in revolt against the old King David. Suffering, death, and destruction came into his family as a punishment of God. Second, the Lord said, "I will raise up evil against thee out of thine own house." Never from this day until his death did David have a peaceful moment, without evil coming from one hand or another. While he was driven from the city of Jerusalem to take refuge in the wilderness from the revolt of his own son Absalom, he was cursed by Shimei, who went along throwing dust in the air and calling him a bloody man. When some of the host wanted to go up and slay Shimei, David said, "Let him alone. The Lord hath told him to curse me. Maybe the Lord will have mercy upon me." David knew that the evil had come to him by way of retribution. Third, God said, "I will take thy wives before thine eyes and give them unto thy neighbor, and it shall be done in the sight of this sun, for thou didst secretly, but I will do this thing before Israel." David had taken another man's wife and secretly violated her, and now the wives of his own household were violated in the eyes of the public by Absalom, his own son. The law of sowing and reaping was completely fulfilled in these characters, David and Bath-sheba. Thus anyone who sins against the Lord by the betrayal of the Lord or the betrayal of a friend or the betrayal of his ideals should tremble with the thought of what God will do to him. Punishment will inevitably come to him in the end. As truly as there is justice and goodness at the heart of the universe, all that is contrary to justice and goodness must either be forgiven through the cross or be punished by suffering.

In a magnificent sermon upon this subject, Dr. C. E. Macartney describes how that the heavenly host were filled with sorrow at the fall of David. The angels refused even the music of their harps during the time between David's fall and David's repentance. One angel said to the other, "Take thine harp and give me melody this day," but the angel answered, "I cannot sing, for David, the man after God's own heart, the man who stole the music of heaven and set it to vibrating among the sons of men, is fallen." But when the tidings came that David had repented and that he had said, "Against Thee, Thee only, have I sinned, and done this evil in Thy sight. Cast me not away from Thy presence; and take not Thy Holy Spirit from me," then there was joy in heaven again. Every harp was lifted and every tongue was loosed in praise of Him Who turns the hearts of kings as waters of rivers are turned. There is joy in heaven over one sinner who repenteth. What joy there must have been over the repentance of David.

You are a woman. Ask yourself tonight whether you have been guilty of sins that will affect others and lead them into temptation and evil. If you are a man, have you ever betrayed another man, or have you betrayed your Lord or the principles of your Lord? If any one of us has sinned in one way or another, have we waited until God should send us another man to convict us of our sin? Why not take the Word as it is given to us tonight and apply it to our hearts, bow in His presence, confessing the evil we have done, and then make restitution thereof before the time of judgment comes? Forgiveness is with Him.

VIII

THE WOMAN WHO MADE A HOUSE A HOME

Jesus loved Martha.

IN a little suburban village not far from a great city stood a fine, old, stone house. The way to this house from the city lay across a valley, up a rather steep incline, through gardens and groves of trees spotted with houses, until it crossed the top of a commanding eminence and began its descent on the other side. Shortly over the brow of the hill, from which could be taken a commanding view of the entire countryside leading for miles in the distance, including the sea itself, was situated this little, pleasant village, with its walled gardens, its lovely trees, its rare flowers, and its beautiful homes. Here merchants and professional people from the city had their residences. Most of these homes were large and spacious, built to remain in the family for years. The particular house in which we are interested had arched ceilings, large doors and hallways, a roof garden, outside porticos, and a private enclosure surrounded by a high wall. This house was forever to be associated with glorious memories.

A house may well be the center of interest not only for the family but also for a nation. When one stands in the Manning Manse, he feels the presence of many generations that have gone before in the long history of that old building. These pioneer colonists, their descendants who were Revolutionists, their descendants who fought in the Civil War, and their descendants who were perhaps at least interested in the outcome of the Great War, with all of the cultural eras that passed between and were reflected in the individual characters of the heads of that household, seem very near to one as he handles the antiques and the relics of other days. It is no wonder that more than two hundred descendants will band themselves together in perpetuity to warrant the upkeep of that house.

Similarly, when one stands in the little home now encased in a national shrine at Hodgenville, Kentucky, he is directly conscious of the presence of Abraham Lincoln, whose early days were spent by the log fire in that home learning his sums of arithmetic and reading his books.

Again, as one stands in the great mansion on the Potomac called "Mount Vernon," he goes back farther still into a period when George and Martha Washington made their great sacrifices for the founding of a nation.

Or as one stands upon the beautiful porch of the columned Monticello at Charlottesville and looks down over the hill to the little law office in which Thomas Jefferson sat and from which he was called to his great office in the service of the country, one feels very close again to the life of a man who laid down principles that have been considered cardinal American principles ever since.

Every home has its story to tell. As one passes through the backwoods of New England and sees the old derelicts that once were inhabited by happy families, which saw their joys and their tragedies, he feels strangely drawn and akin to another generation. Thus it is when one stands before the ruins of the old home in the village of Bethany.

There came a day when sorrow stalked through this particular house, when friends and relatives gathered to comfort the widow of the head of the household, when days of mourning were finished, and when the dear woman walked about those gardens and through those halls and chambers with a sense of loneliness that nothing could drive away. It was during these dark and dreary hours that the widow heard of a religious Teacher Who gave beautiful sayings to His followers and Who they claimed was able to comfort their hearts with a comfort that they could never know in any other way. One day she left her home and went to Jerusalem and stood at the edge of the multitude and listened to Him talk and heard Him say, "Come unto Me, all ye that labor and are heavy laden, and I will give you rest." She heard Him tell that He had come to bind up the broken-hearted, that His Father in heaven was interested in the least one who suffered, even in a sparrow who fell to the ground, and that nothing could occur to them, not even the falling of a hair from their heads, without His knowledge. Something within her heart responded, and she determined that this Man should be her Rabbi, her Teacher. As the days went on, she not only believed in Him and accepted His teachings concerning Himself as the Messiah, the sent One of Israel, but she also led her younger sister and her brother, all that she had left of her dear ones in the world, to a faith in Him such as was hers.

Up until this profession of her faith and this committal of her life unto the Teacher she had not known what to do with her great home on the hill, but now she caught a vision of what that home could do. She would dedicate it to this Messiah and to His disciples as a place of refreshment and rest, as a retreat for teaching, as a gathering place for those who would listen and who would follow Him more closely. What wonderful stories might be told of the houses owned by widows, which have been dedicated to Christ, to the church, and to the work of the kingdom of God, of the groups who have gathered there to learn, to study the Bible, to hear the Word from some spiritual leader! How many have entered the hospitality of such homes to be changed in their inner characters and to go forth with faith into the world! All too little do we make use of our homes as places for the growth of the church and the influence of the Lord Jesus Christ, yet how sanctified are those few houses dedicated to these ends! What about that house of yours, that white elephant, that great derelict? Have you ever dedicated it unto God and to God's work? Have you turned it over to the use of those who are the people of God for service? That house may become one of the centers of God's influence in your community.

That is exactly what this home at Bethany became. So we invite you to look at the *Home Over Which Martha Presided,* then at the *Home of Martha in Sorrow,* then, at the *Home of Martha in Joy.* We mention all this that you may remember Jesus in just such a setting on the day in which we think of Him as King.

I. THE HOME OVER WHICH MARTHA PRESIDED

There were many houses in and around Jerusalem, but only one of them was home for Jesus. When Jesus thought of Capernaum, home was the house of Peter's mother-in-law, who had made Him welcome when He had been driven from Nazareth. When He thought of home at Cana of Galilee, it was the home of Nathanael. Whenever He thought of home near Jerusalem, it was the house of Martha in Bethany. Nothing in this house was good enough for the Master, in Martha's eyes. Whenever the announcement was made, "The Master cometh," Martha felt that all hands must go to work to make the necessary arrangements.

And the Master came whenever He was tired and weary and in need of sympathy—the touch of a woman's hand. Men who are in public life, in conflict, in strife, under criticism, bearing burdens of others, love the place called home. It is their castle, their fortress, their resting-place, and happy are they when a good woman makes it a true home. Whenever the scribes and Pharisees and doctors of the law made life difficult for Jesus in Jerusalem, by questioning Him and ridiculing Him and pouring their contempt upon Him, and when His tender humanity ached with sorrow and suffering, and when He was exceedingly burdened with the sins of those with whom He discoursed and for whom He labored, He walked out at eventide to Bethany, over the crown of the Mount of Olives, and there in Martha's house He found a haven of rest. This privilege of going to a place that shuts out the din and the harshness of the world, where love abides and where one is surrounded with those who are sympathetically and affectionately inclined, is one of the precious experiences of life. It is no wonder that Jesus loved the home of Martha of Bethany and that He habitually frequented it whenever He was in the vicinity of Jerusalem. Especially is this true when we realize that it is written of the Son of God that He had no place to lay His head. He was rejected in His own city. He was utterly dependent upon the kindness and the hospitality of friends. He often slept out-of-doors in the wilderness, wrapped only in His outer cloak, and when He approached Jerusalem, it was with joy that He thought of the home of Martha.

This hospitality of Martha for Christ is the New Testament counterpart of the Shunammite's hospitality for the prophet Elisha in the Old Testament. If you recall, the prophet was in the habit of passing her door in his travels from Mount Carmel to Jezreel. So she inquired of her husband if it were not possible for them to prepare a chamber in the wall that might be called The Prophet's Chamber and where he might turn in at his own leisure and rest as he willed in passing. There she put simple furniture, such as a chair, a bed, and a table, and there the prophet stopped from time to time in his journey. Then there came the time of her need, when the son who had been born to her in fulfillment of the prophet's word fell on a day and died. The reward came to the Shunammite woman for her interest in and hospitality to the prophet. She made known her dire need unto him and through the prophet's intercession with God, the child was restored to her, well. In detail there is a great parallelism between this Old Testament story and the story of Martha, for Martha's brother Lazarus, probably also a younger person, fell sick and Martha sent for Christ, as the Shunammite woman sent for

Elisha, and when Christ came, though too late for any earthly help, He raised Lazarus from the dead. This was the fruit of her hospitality.

The first mention we have of Martha is in connection with a dinner party she prepared for Jesus and probably for some of His disciples. The Lord was on His way from Capernaum to Jerusalem, and He passed by Bethany and turned in to the house of Martha, who received Him gladly. We are not told whether the disciples were entertained or not, but we suppose that they were. Thus it was that a great burden devolved upon Martha and upon her servants in order to prepare the evening meal. While Jesus was resting, she went about overseeing the directions in the home. The rooms were being straightened, the dinner was being prepared, the servants were hustling hither and yon, and Martha was bearing the full responsibility of all that she called the service. It was no easy task in a day of no delicatessens to prepare suddenly for unexpected guests. The words that describe Martha's condition are, "Cumbered about much serving." She had been bustling about from the time that Jesus arrived until nearly the time of the dinner. She was more tired than she knew, and her judgment was hardly clear. Her judgment was that of a woman overwrought, highly strung, and in a nervous state, typical of one who had worked too hard and now tried all the harder because of her own condition. Surely there is nothing to condemn in this. There is nothing reproachful. In fact, the woman was quite commendable, and whatever weakness or irritability rested in her was due to her physical condition rather than to her spiritual state. It was at this moment that the incident occurred which has left Martha's reputation somewhat in doubt in the church.

Throughout the day she had noticed that Mary, her younger sister, had done nothing but wait upon Christ and had sat at His feet to listen to Him as He taught and to ask Him many questions that seemed to her to be of a speculative nature and altogether unnecessary when so much was to be done, and yet she condoned her and allowed her to continue in her interests until almost the hour arrived for the dinner. Then, as she passed by Mary and Jesus once more, for some unknown reason she felt provoked at her and interrupted their quiet talk with a rude question, saying, "Master, carest Thou not that my sister hath left me to serve alone? Bid her, therefore, that she help me." How many times this particular incident could be repeated in almost every home! Yet Jesus, knowing perfectly the spiritual condition and the life of both women, quietly responded, "Martha, Martha, thou art careful and troubled about many things; but one thing is needful, and Mary hath chosen that good part which shall not be taken away from her." We remember that when the Apostles in the early church became cumbered about much serving of the tables, it occurred to them that it was not meet that they should leave the Word of God and do this work. Therefore, they appointed deacons who were ordained to accomplish this task. Wherever a minister of the Word of God leaves his primary task to take up the secondary task of serving, even though they be matters of charity and of common kindness, he nevertheless is not doing a commendable thing. He has not chosen the best part.

Martha's work was just as necessary as the work Mary performed, and Jesus did not tell her not to do that work. He did not rebuke her for doing it. He merely emphasized that one work was better than another. Every housewife or housemaid who does her work as unto the Lord is serving the Lord Jesus Christ. Every man in his carpenter shop or in his business may be serving the Lord Jesus Christ there just as well as someone else whom the Lord has delegated to a different field is serving Him there. Dr. Abraham Kuiper says that in the church of Christ some busy themselves with silver, others with gold, and still others with mere wood and stone, using Paul's expression. We can say that the difference between Mary and Martha is that the former worked in gold and the latter in silver, but certainly all are not to work in gold, for he who works in silver is doing his duty. Supposing John the Evangelist to be one who worked in pure gold and Mark to be one who worked in silver, Mark would have been shirking his responsibility had he attempted to imitate John in the teaching he recorded. Thus it is here also. God placed two sisters in Lazarus' family, and He gave them appropriate talents, and accordingly had given to each a peculiar calling. For that reason, each acquitted herself of her responsibility only when she followed her own particular path. In His reprimand of Martha, Jesus did not tell her to do as Mary did, but when Martha valued her own silver more highly than Mary's gold, when she told Jesus, "Tell Mary to assist me in serving," then Jesus felt that she had to be enlightened. It was then that He told her that Mary had not chosen to do the less desirable but the more desirable thing. Martha had no right to look with disdain upon Mary's quiet, peaceful, faith-engendered spiritual life, and those who follow the pathway of Mary have no right to look down upon Martha with disdain. Both occupations are desirable. It is highly blessed that we have some who are engaged in deeds of mercy, but it is also necessary that some be engaged in the work of the kingdom of God, which is the direct preaching of the gospel of Jesus Christ, and each in his place is best. Martha in her own place was certainly supreme.

II. THE HOME OF MARTHA IN SORROW

Suffering plays a large part in making a house a home. When a family moves into a new home, it is highly improbable that it will ever feel quite as much at home in the new house until it has had some session of illness, some crisis, or some experience of need. Then it is that the walls seem to enter into one's own experience to sympathize with one and to partake of his life. Perhaps some of us are

The Woman Who Made a House a Home   115

more sentimental about a house than others, but as Edgar Guest says, "It takes a heap o' living to make a house a home." When you have planted the shrubbery that grows around your house and tended the garden and raised the blades of grass, when you have built the stone wall that encases your garden, when you have enclosed your porch, when you have entertained in your livingroom, when you have cleaned it and remodeled it year after year, and when you have sat through the long quiet hours of the night waiting by the side of the bed of some loved one, whether mother or daughter, until the morning light should break upon a face that would respond for the better or for the worse, that house becomes a home. When the suffering and the living and the loving seem to saturate its very walls and fill it with a heap of memories, it becomes a place that wherever you are in the world you will always look back to and call home. Perhaps Mother is no longer there. Perhaps sister has long since been married and brother gone away, but still it is home. Can you forget the mental picture drawn by Margaret Mitchell of Scarlett O'Hara returning to her home, Tara, after Sherman's invasion of Georgia and the burning of the great mansions along the way, only to find the stock gone, the furniture stolen, the barns burned, and nothing but the bare building yet standing? Still as she stood upon the barren ground and looked across the hills at the noble building, she cried, "Tara," for it was home. Either cottage or a mansion, however humble, "there is no place like home."

Now came the time of suffering and sorrow for the household at Bethany, during which Martha's protective strength was revealed. The story in the eleventh chapter of John is one of the touching and beautiful in the Scripture. Here we even learn that Jesus wept, and here Martha stands out with the majesty of a woman who knew how to conduct herself in the time of trouble and trial. The day came when Lazarus did not rise from his bed in the morning, when he called for his sisters and told them that he did not feel well. They tended him as many others have tended loved ones, thinking that their loved one was slightly ill and would soon be better, but as the days passed they soon saw that it was not as minor an ailment as they had supposed but rather that Lazarus was rapidly slipping down-hill. Then it was, in the fear which was almost a premonition, that they thought of the Lord Jesus and decided to send to Him. The message was terse and short, only, "Lord, behold he whom Thou lovest is sick," but it was sufficient to tell the story. These women knew that if Jesus could come all would be well with their brother.

For some reason into which we do not need to enter for the purpose of this discussion, Jesus tarried for several days after the message came to Him in the section called Perea. Then, when He knew that Lazarus was dead, He turned His face toward Bethany. Meanwhile, we may well imagine how that Mary and Martha alternately took turns watching by the bedside of Lazarus and going to their portico to look down the long road toward Jericho to see if Jesus were coming or if any company that might be the company of Jesus were on its way. Then the time came when Martha, weeping, made her way out to her sister Mary, standing looking toward the east, and broke the news that Lazarus was dead.

Four days passed, during which they and their friends had Lazarus embalmed and buried in the cave not far from their home on the hill. Then, with much misgiving, they waited and waited for the coming of Jesus. During this time Martha recovered more quickly than Mary, for as soon as she heard that Jesus was coming, she went and met Him, but Mary sat still in the house, buried in her grief and in her mourning. When Martha came to Jesus, she said, "Lord, if Thou hadst been here my brother had not died, but I know that even now whatsoever Thou wilt ask of God, God will give it Thee." What a remarkable faith

The Woman Who Made a House a Home

that is! What a triumphant statement! What a confession to the Lord! Her faith was so great that Jesus merely said, "Thy brother shall rise again." Then Martha replied (and note the "I know"), "I know that he shall rise again in the resurrection at the last day." Here was a woman with a certainty of faith that declared that she had not seen the last of her brother and that they would be united once again. But Jesus said, "I am the resurrection and the life. He that believeth in Me, though he were dead, yet shall he live; and whosoever liveth and believeth in Me shall never die. Believest thou this?" Still in faith, Martha said, "Yes, Lord, I believe that Thou art the Christ, the Son of God which should come into the world." Here we catch a vision of a woman who had as great a faith and who made as great a statement of that faith as any disciple made before the resurrection of Christ. She believed, and she was ready to act upon that belief.

We have no record that Jesus spoke and asked for Mary, but we read that Martha went to Mary and said to her, "The Master is come and calleth for thee." This we take to be some of the protective kindness Martha manifested toward her sister Mary during these days, for the news of the arrival of the Lord Jesus and that He wanted her caused Mary to go into His presence immediately. There she, too, said what Martha had said, "Lord, if Thou hadst been here my brother had not died," and with that she left her confession and broke into weeping. Surely it was this suffering of Mary as much as anything else that caused the tears to come from the eyes of our blessed Lord, even though He knew that He was to raise Lazarus from the dead. Thus it was that these women received the answer to their faith. At the command of the Lord, the stone was rolled away from the grave and, though Martha protested that already decay had set in, Jesus spoke, "Lazarus, come forth." Then the greatest miracle of all that were performed by Christ occurred—the body of the man Lazarus came forth, bound hand and foot with grave clothes, and his face covered about with a napkin, and Jesus commanded those standing around about to loose him and let him go. Lazarus, a dead man, was raised to life again. The scene of reunion and joy can only be imagined and not described.

III. The Home of Martha in Joy

The last picture we get of Martha and of her home is on the day preceding the triumphal entry of Christ into Jerusalem, as King. It was on the Sabbath evening before the Passover, when Christ was again entertained at Bethany with a dinner party in the home of Simon the leper, at which Martha had control of the serving. This undoubtedly is the same home, being the home of Martha, but now called by the name of her late husband. The central personage of interest at this dinner was Lazarus who, the record tells us twice, was the one who had been dead, whom Christ had raised from the dead. Lazarus was the standing miracle who was convincing the Jews constantly that Jesus was the Christ, their Messiah. This time, not only Jesus was present but all of His disciples. Together with Lazarus they sat at this large table partaking of the feast. We have no means of knowing what the conversation was at this particular dinner, but we may be sure that it included such topics as "the spiritual meaning of the Passover" which was soon to be celebrated, whereby the Lord God had provided for the people of God a means of atonement for the forgiveness of their sins. It probably included that great subject of prayer about which the disciples had asked the Lord the last time they had visited at Bethany, when they said, "Lord, teach us to pray." It may even have included some suggestions by Christ of the approaching end of His own life, their concern about it, and their failure to understand the cause of His death. Did Lazarus tell them about his experience during death, or did he find that all such former experiences were forgotten when he returned into this world? We

The Woman Who Made a House a Home 119

have no means of knowing, but we know that he must have conversed with them because of the prominence given to him as one who sat at the table. In him the disciples had evidence enough to seal their faith in Christ regardless of whatever occurred in the future, knowing that He was God's messenger, God's Son.

In this memorable season of the Passover, Martha gave her expression of gratitude and celebration of the raising of her brother Lazarus and the restoring of him to her home in the presentation of this great feast. Once again we find her building with her works of silver rather than works of gold. To how much of the conversation Martha listened we do not know, but we know that she served. This time it does not tell that she was cumbered about much serving. Martha now performed the work to which God had called her without the unnecessary nervous excitability. Let all the Marthas in the church take comfort in the fact that the Lord acknowledges their service and that the Lord accepts their service. The matter most important to Him is how the service is performed, whether in peace and in faith or in turmoil and unbelief.

Mary's expression of gratitude was different from Martha's. Mary had probably thought a long time what she could do. Her sister was giving the great dinner. Lazarus could sit at the table and express himself to the Lord Jesus, but Mary had no talent at all except that of listening, so Mary took the costly ointment that had been purchased, perhaps at the price of her savings, brought the alabaster container into the great room during the feast, and there cracked the box and poured the ointment over His feet so that the aroma filled the house with pleasant odors. Then she proceeded to wipe His feet with her hair and to caress them with her hands. Hers was to be a service of adoration and of worship. In fact, one surmises that Mary had a premonition of the coming death of Christ, or at least that she acted in faith upon His own teaching that He was soon to die. That Mary was rebuked by Judas and the disciples is beside the point here, for they did not understand. But Jesus did, and He said, "Let her alone: against the day of My burying hath she kept this. Wherever this gospel shall be preached throughout the whole world this also that she hath done shall be spoken of for a memorial of her." Truly, wherever the gospel has been preached we have remembered Mary for her act of adoration and love, but we have also remembered Martha for her act of courtesy and hospitality and love to her Lord. One was as great as the other within the sphere of each life.

Happy is it that we may remember Jesus on the first day of the last week in such a setting as this, among His friends, among loved ones, among disciples. We see Him present in and blessing the house of those whom He loved. Thereafter, Martha, Mary, and Lazarus could always say, "Christ is the Head of this house, the unseen Guest at every meal, the silent listener to every conversation," for Christ was really there.

Have you invited Jesus Christ into your home? Is the house in which you live the home of the Lord? Because He dwells in you, does He dwell there? Do you begin the day with Him, either in family worship or at least grace at the table? Have you honored Him in all things, and do you obey Him and follow His guidance during the day? Do you minister unto Him, and do you sit at His feet to worship Him? If you accept Jesus into your home, you will find that sometimes He will rebuke you for your choice of the lesser instead of the better thing, but He will love you in the midst of it all and in His gentleness He will make your house a heavenly home on earth until you may go to the Father's house in which there are many mansions, one prepared for you.

IX
THE WOMAN WHO COULD NOT FORGET

On the first day of the week cometh Mary Magdalene early, when it was yet dark, to the sepulcher.

OF all the women in the Bible, the highest place, next to Mary the Virgin, must be accorded to Mary Magdalene. She took the most prominent part and is given the most prominent place in the Passion narratives of our Lord. She takes this high place because she could never forget what Jesus Christ had done for her.

Women who cannot forget are often trouble-makers. They cannot overlook nor forget slights or wrongs that have been done to them, or even opposition to their will. Their desire for vengeance causes incalculable suffering in the world. Remember Jezebel's determination to be avenged of Elijah, and the anger of Herodias at Baptist John, ending in his death!

Other women, however, can never forget the good that is done to them; they always want to repay that good and become a blessing to the world. Such a woman was the wife of Chuza, Herod's steward, whose name was Joanna. She had been cured by our Lord, either of possession by an evil spirit or of a disease, and out of her gratitude she attached herself to that body of women who accompanied Him upon His journeys and ministered to Him of their substance and who were faithful to the cross and even to the resurrection morning, for she came with Mary Magdalene to the tomb to anoint the body with spices. Another is Martha, whose life we have already studied and who because of the Lord's goodness to her family, including the raising of Lazarus from the dead, could never do enough for Him by way of service. But greater than either of these is the one who is the subject of our discourse, namely, Mary Magdalene.

Of all the grateful women in the Bible who could not forget, Mary Magdalene is the outstanding person. Therefore, she may stand for us as the symbol of the worship of the Christ by women who cannot forget what Christ has done for them. Hers is the single case that presents the resurrection in all of its historic and its spiritual phases to us. In her own life we see the spiritual resurrection from a life condemned to bondage and through her eyes we can see the physical resurrection of Christ. Centering our attention upon Mary and the part she played in the resurrection, may I suggest for your consideration, first, *What Mary Could Not Forget;* second, *The Person Whom Mary Could Not Forget;* and third, *What Mary Would Have Missed Had She Forgotten.*

I. WHAT MARY COULD NOT FORGET

We are introduced to Mary Magdalene in the verses immediately following the story of Jesus and the woman who was a sinner. This has resulted in Mary often being identified with the woman who was a sinner, but the Scripture only says that Mary had been healed of evil spirits and infirmities, seven devils going out from her. Thus there are three theories concerning Mary's past.

The first theory identifies Mary with the sinful woman. In the great Zwinger Gallery in Dresden, there is a picture by Coreggio of the Magdalene. She lies in a cave, still marked by the badges of her sin but now reading from the Scripture. Her long tresses fall about her full neck and exposed bosom, with every indication given of voluptuous practices from which she has just now been snatched. Before her appearance has changed, with the exception of the look in her eyes, she has her attention riveted upon the Scripture. The idea portrayed is that Mary was the woman who was a sinner and had only now returned to a lonely place to be confirmed in the change wrought by Jesus at the feast of Simon. This conception of Mary is quite general in the Christian world, so that the word "Magdalene" has come to represent a fallen woman; we have houses of Magdalene, homes for such poor souls who are victims of social evil. The Roman Church has done more than any other influence to fasten this stigma upon Mary by the means of the practice of a very worthy charity. Beginning in the fourteenth century, they established a series of monasteries called "Magdalen Houses," in each of which were three congregations, those of St. Magdalen, those of St. Martha, and those of St. Lazarus, which reveals the Roman identification of Mary Magdalene, the fallen woman, and Mary of Bethany as one person. There may be some question about the identification of the fallen woman and Mary of Bethany, but certainly this fallen woman cannot be Mary Magdalene. Since that date, Magdalen houses have been established all over the world.

Though Roman Catholicism identifies Mary Magdalene and the woman who was a sinner, most Protestant scholars give good grounds for not identifying them. Certainly a woman who was demon possessed is not one who would be profitable in that oldest trade of the world. That fallen woman was saved at a house of Simon, the Pharisee, who had invited Jesus and His disciples to a feast, but had omitted all of the common courtesies and amenities of the social order, such as the kiss of salutation, the water for the washing of the feet, and the oil for the anointing of the head. During the feast, this woman of the streets entered and made her way directly to the couch of Jesus. Simon did not stop her, thinking that probably Christ would, but Christ paid her no attention. She must have been touched somewhere by some of His teaching and have had her heart changed, and now she came to express her gratitude to Him. Kneeling by His couch, she washed His feet with her tears and wiped them with the hairs of her head and then anointed them with precious oil, which undoubtedly was purchased of the reward of her iniquity and consumed much of her substance. Jesus then used the incident as a parable to teach the unforgiving and supercilious Simon a lesson. He said: "There was a certain creditor which had two debtors; the one owed five hundred pence and the other fifty, and when they had nothing to pay, he frankly forgave them both. Tell me, therefore, which of them will love him most?" Simon replied, "I suppose that he to whom he forgave most." Jesus then said, "Thou hast rightly judged" and, turning to the woman, He continued, "Seest thou this woman? I entered thine house and thou gavest Me no water for My feet, but she hath washed My feet with tears and wiped them with the hairs of her head. Thou gavest Me no kiss; but this woman since the time I came in hath not ceased to kiss My feet. My head with oil thou didst not anoint: but this woman hath anointed My feet with ointment. Wherefore I say unto thee, her sins, which are many, are forgiven; for she loved much: but to whom little is forgiven, the same loveth little." Then to the woman He said, "Thy faith hath saved thee; go in peace." Whether this woman was Mary or not, which only heaven can reveal, she believed on the Lord Jesus Christ and that belief was the source of love that was poured out upon Him, in due humility. Perhaps we are wrong and this woman was Mary Magdalene. If so, all honor to her as she abandoned her illicit and shameful trade and became a true follower of the Lord Jesus Christ.

The second interpretation, and that to which we adhere, is that Mary was a lunatic and demon possessed. Rather than a fallen woman, we think of her as an afflicted woman, suffering from an unfortunate condition prevalent in Jesus' day. When we recall the story of the demoniac of Gadara, which was just across the lake from Magdala, where tradition says there were many demon possessed and where

The Woman Who Could Not Forget 125

Christ healed at least one who had lived naked and who had broken his chains and dwelt among the caves, and frightened all comers, we have a picture of what Mary must have been like. Think of this woman of delicate frame, now irrational and with lunatic outlook, with wild eyes and disheveled hair, either living in the tombs or haunting the outskirts of the village until Jesus found her. If you would see people like that today, go to the insane asylums, listen to their wails, see their senseless, raving eyes, listen to their talk, watch them leap, dance, or crawl, and you will have an idea of what Mary was like. Whether demon possession was the same as insanity or a particular manifestation of the evil world at the same time that heaven put forth its best and sent Jesus into the world, we cannot be sure, but out of Mary went seven demons. Perhaps men had driven her, as many weaker vessels in our day have been driven to insanity, by cruelty. A domineering father, a thoughtless husband, exposure to extreme calamity, or some other cause may have lain back of it, but the people of Magdala called her "Mary" in scorn, as the town crazy woman, but when Jesus first saw her and realized what this woman in her rational condition would become, He said, "Mary," in a different way, which she could never forget. Into her dim, distant look there came focused reason and understanding, followed by a balanced appreciation and love. Mary was healed and was returned, clothed, and in her right mind, to her home and family. No wonder that Mary's gratitude to the Lord Jesus was great!

There is yet a third interpretation of the history of Mary, which is advanced by Dr. MacLaren. He believed that these seven demons were figurative representations of the seven sins of Dante, which are to be found in the hearts of us all, and that Mary was neither a great sinner nor was she a maniac, but that she was perfectly delivered in this world from the evil that hounds each of us, namely, pride, envy, anger, lasciviousness, covetousness, intemperance, and spiritual sloth. That old Scottish preacher testified that he could never find those demons completely vanished from his heart and life and that anyone so delivered must have been a great saint. Mary became just such a saint. If this interpretation is true, it is the correct interpretation of the power of Christ to quicken us from our trespasses and sins to a new life. This kind of resurrection, we all need to know. What Jesus did for Mary, He has done for multitudes throughout history.

It is quite clear that whatever the original condition of Mary, she was thoroughly and completely changed by the power of Christ. If she was a lunatic, then the first time that Jesus said, "Mary," her reason returned to her and she looked out upon the world with rational and with sensible eyes and countenance. If she was a sinner of the streets, then when Jesus told her, "Go in peace; thy faith hath saved thee," a transformation occurred that was a mighty miracle. If through listening to His teaching she was delivered from the mortal sins that plague the lives of most people, she stands as a monument of the grace of God. Whatever Mary's past, her change is an illustration of a spiritual resurrection in the life of an individual. Paul said, "You who were dead in trespasses and sins hath He quickened," and then he calls this a resurrection. Undoubtedly it is a resurrection, but it is not the only resurrection. There later arose some in the church who claimed that this was the only resurrection and that the resurrection spoken of in the Bible was just for those who are Christians, but Paul declared it to be an error. However, we may know this great, spiritual resurrection. This is the demonstration that Christ is living today. Whenever a character is changed, whenever a sinner is transformed from the kingdom of darkness to the kingdom of light, when habits are broken and a new life begins, we have evidence of the fact that Christ has risen from the dead and is living.

The Woman Who Could Not Forget 127

Immediately after Mary was changed, she entered upon a ministry of gratitude to Christ. She joined the little group of women who, as Matthew says, "ministered unto Him of their substance." Very probably Mary came from a family of much substance and now she not only dedicated her person but she dedicated her possessions to Him and to His servants. Christ and His disciples had to live in some way, and these women probably provided the means for their sustenance. It would be well to follow Mary's example, for we can certainly do no better when Christ has bestowed upon us spiritual and moral healing than to give both ourselves and our possessions to Him as gifts upon His altar. Mary did not cease her ministry with the giving of her substance. She also devoted her service to Christ. Mary was faithful to Him when all others failed. The narrative implies that she was the inspiring spirit among all of the faithful women, for she is always named first in the group, whether at the cross or at the tomb, by all of the evangelists. When others had fled from Christ at the time of His capture and then of His trial, proving that they could not stand with Him, Mary proved that she could. When the morning light dawned on that Day of the Passover and the multitudes assembled at the Gabbatha, word came to Mary that the Master was arrested and was being accused before Pilate. Thither she went with all haste to witness, to help, and to encourage Jesus, but helpless, she stood back on the edge of the scene, prevented by the soldiers from coming nearer. It was there that she saw all of the events that led to Golgotha, but there was no fear on Mary's part. Even at the cross, when others mocked Him and ridiculed Him and probably were very hostile to any followers who might be there, yet Mary stayed. When Jesus sent His own mother, Mary the Virgin, away with John the Beloved, still Mary Magdalene remained. Rubens, in one of his great paintings, depicts Mary as helping Joseph of Arimathea and Nicodemus to remove Christ's body from the cross and participating in the labors of love as it was bound and prepared for burial. Then she followed the little procession to the tomb and observed all that was done, weeping. She and Mary, the mother of Joseph, particularly marked where the body was laid and how the tomb was closed before they left because of the coming of the Sabbath, which they must spend in their homes.

Never was a sadder Sabbath spent in the history of the world than that when the Son of God lay in the tomb, and during this Sabbath, Mary was occupied not only with sorrow and remembering but also with the preparing of a love gift that she might again minister to her Lord on the first day of the week. Then she and the women returned to the tomb to perform a deed of gratitude and affection as the last symbol of her loyalty. Mary impresses one as desiring that her life should adequately express her gratitude. This may have been unconscious and natural to her, but it nevertheless was present. Surely every Christian should examine his own life according to his profession of benefit and blessing from the Lord to see if he has forgotten those things in the action he manifests before the world.

II. THE PERSON WHOM SHE COULD NOT FORGET

One of the strange things about bereavement is that when we have lost a loved one, the particular characteristics of that person stand out more clearly than they did when he was living. We can remember one particular thing he was in the habit of doing or one particular expression that endeared him to us. Such thoughts must have occupied Mary's meditation on the Sabbath. She probably thought of the person of the human Jesus, of His sufferings on the cross, and of the transformation He had wrought in her life and that was the first impression she had of Him.

There is no doubt that Mary was interested in the human Jesus. The prophet Isaiah said, "There is no beauty that we should desire Him." Others could not see the beauty that was in Jesus, but Mary saw that beauty, and she loved it and Him. To Mary, Jesus was truly the Lily of the Valley, the Rose of Sharon, the Bright and Morning Star. He was the sunrise and the sunset of her soul. The dignity, the authority, the mercy, the kindness, and the endless service Christ performed in utter devotion to the will of God had utterly captivated Mary. She was enthralled with Him. Life without Jesus for Mary was meaningless. It was not worth living. It was empty and void. It was worse than useless. Mary loved in Christ that which others hated, namely, His perfect goodness and righteousness. It is in this way that Christ reveals the character of persons. If His perfection and His righteousness call forth your love and your affection, happy are you, but if it calls forth your hatred and your repugnance, woe unto you, for then you are full of sin. Sinful men do not love Christ, for His perfections show up their imperfections.

It is perfectly possible that the fleshly Christ may have been too much in Mary's mind, but how could she separate the two? She was devoted to His body from beginning to end, so that when she once saw the resurrected Christ, she fell at His feet, wishing to clasp them to her again, now to keep Him forever, for Mary was unable to distinguish between the spiritual and the physical Christ.

Thus we may understand the sorrow of Mary in her sense of loss at the death of Jesus. Her woman's mind did not think of what it meant to the cause, that Jesus had died. She had no interest in the kingdom, as the disciples did, or in power, or in politics, or the breaking of the Roman yoke. She was interested only in fellowship, and love, and communion. His death interrupted her fellowship, and she was overwhelmed with the sense that she would see Him no more, and this was too much for her. Mary simply could not get her mind away from the tomb in which the body of Christ reposed. She loved Jesus, and now Jesus was dead. Thus Mary's love lingered on the body of Christ. Perhaps you cannot understand that now, but some day you will, in the hour of bereavement. Few are the emancipated souls that can love the spirit of the person disassociated from the body. Mary had not reached that high position yet.

On that Sabbath Day, the remembrance of the sufferings of Christ on the cross must have weighed on Mary. She had seen everything, from the trial at the Gabbatha to the tomb. She saw all those events, His mock trial, His refusal to defend Himself, Pilate publicly washing his hands to clear himself of the guilt, the result of the scourging as they thrust Him forth bleeding and crowned with thorns, saying, "Behold the Man." Surely if ever Mary wept, it was then. Mary followed as near as possible outside the ring of soldiers as they led Him along the Via Dolorosa to crucify Him. She was one of those weeping women to whom Jesus turned and said as He went along, "Daughters of Jerusalem, weep not for Me, but weep for yourselves ... for if they do these things in a green tree, what shall be done in a dry?" Mary had seen Him fall under the cross, receive the lashes from the soldiers, but, unable to go on, transfer His burden to Simon the Cyrenian. Then she had stood by the cross during the entire crucifixion and saw Him in agony. Mary could not forget the words He had spoken there, words praying for the forgiveness of His crucifiers and tormentors, words of promise to a dying thief, words of petition unto a Father Who seemed not to hear. Yes, Mary was burdened by the sufferings of the person of Christ.

Moreover, she knew these to be unjust. She knew that He had never wronged a soul and that He was hated only because He freed men from the yoke of the law, from fear, from disease, as she had been freed. She was sure in her own mind that He never claimed to be a King of anything but of truth and of righteousness. He even refused to be made king when they wanted to force Him to become King. He was no rival of Caesar, not even of the high priest, and yet His friends and His followers and all those whom He had helped and healed and befriended had deserted Him. Why such events were permitted to happen troubled Mary severely, just as they have troubled many who have seen the just suffer ever since the cross. It is possible that the vicariousness of the Calvary may have faintly dawned upon Mary's mind, but she had no certainty of it. Only the thought that Jesus was dying for sinful men as their substitute, bearing their sin and the penalty of their evil, the curse of the law, can explain the cross, and only the vicariousness of the suffering of the righteous is able to place meaning into it today. We are able, because of the cross of Christ, to endure that which we are called upon to endure when we innocently suffer.

No doubt much of that day was also spent in remembrance of what this Person had wrought in her life. She vividly sensed the peace, the joy, and the purpose that had been substituted for her aimless, distracted, tumultuous living of other days. How blessed it had been to walk with Him during these three years! Was it all to end now? Was she again to be enmeshed in her sin, in her failures, in her evil, in her distractions of mind, and in her sorrow? Now that He was dead, was she again to go back to the old life? No, a thousand times no! She would now live as if He were with her always. Nevertheless, there was a very real fear with Mary that if Jesus were dead and remained dead, He could no longer deliver her from her present enemies, from evil within and without, and in that Mary was right. It is folly to think that anything but a resurrected, living Christ can give deliverance from sin today. If Jesus remained in the tomb, or if His body was stolen by anyone and did not rise from the dead, then Christ is not a deliverer; then He has not defeated our great enemy and we have real reason to fear. Mary sensed the fact that a dead Jesus would declare the cross to be a defeat and the end of the cause, both for her and for the Christian movement, and so it would.

III. What Mary Would Have Missed Had She Forgotten

Had Mary not been the grateful woman she was, she would have missed many things. First of all, she would have missed the revelation of the resurrected Christ. But Mary did not forget and was the first in faithfulness and hence, the first in reward, for unto Mary, Christ first appeared after His resurrection. Wonderful were those events of that first Easter morning, and in them all Mary played a prominent part. She came with Mary of Galilee and Joanna and other women following, bearing the spices that they might anoint the body of Jesus, and worrying over who should move the stone for them. When they came to the tomb, saw the soldiers overcome and lying upon the ground, an angel sitting upon the stone, and heard the words, "He is not here, but risen; go and tell His disciples," like a flash Mary turned and went to tell Peter and John, while Mary of Galilee went on to the women, who in turn came to investigate the tomb and then left in order to inform the rest of the disciples. Meanwhile Mary, Peter, and John returned to the tomb to see what had happened to the body of Jesus. Peter entered, and I suppose the others followed, where they saw the linen clothes lying and the napkin folded, and John believed Jesus had risen from the dead. After the disciples left, Mary was alone, weeping and wondering what had happened to the body of Jesus. She did not yet believe either the message of the angels or the evidence that her Lord was risen. Then it was that she saw someone approaching her whom she took to be the gardener, and not recognizing Him through her tears, she asked, "If thou hast taken Him away, tell me and I will take Him." Suddenly she heard a Voice say, "Mary!" She knew it was the voice of her Lord. She fell at His feet to grasp Him and hold Him forever, now that He had been restored to her. Surely this Mary was no more mistaken

The Woman Who Could Not Forget 133

in her vision of the resurrected Christ than were the other disciples in His later appearances. She went to the disciples later in the day and affirmed that it was even so, that the resurrected Lord had appeared to her. Whatever you may think about the resurrection, these appearances of Christ cannot be reasoned away. They were seen by too many people, in too many places, and too many different times in order to be treated lightly.

While Mary sat at Jesus' feet, an incident occurred that presents the Christian conception of Christ. He said to her, "Touch Me not, for I am not yet ascended, but go to My disciples and tell them I go before them into Galilee. I ascend unto My Father and to your Father." How shall we interpret this passage, which says, "Touch Me not," when a few moments later seemingly Christ allowed the other women to touch Him? Some say that Mary would have clung to the body to keep Jesus with her forever, to hold this fleshly knowledge and experience. Mary needed gentle instruction that Christ was about to assume a new relationship and that she should not seek to hold Him to this earth. Paul once said, "Though we have known Christ after the flesh, yea, now, henceforth know we Him no more." It is possible to have a fleshly knowledge of Christ and to have a spiritual knowledge of Christ. When Paul held the fleshly knowledge, he persecuted Jesus. When he had the spiritual knowledge, he loved Him and served Him as a disciple. In the flesh, Christ could be with only one person at one place at one time, but the ascended Christ is omnipresent and with us always. Augustine suggested that now we should touch Him with the hands of faith and not with the hands of the flesh.

Another thing that Mary would have missed had she forgotten, was being commissioned as the first messenger of the resurrected Lord. She was the first to hear the heavenly tidings of the gospel completed with the resurrection. This gospel vindicated by the resurrection is the greatest message that ever was committed to man and was ever preached. Paul told Timothy to be unashamed of the gospel of Christ because he could remember that God raised Him from the dead. With the resurrection there is no need ever to be ashamed of this great gospel, for it is vindicated before the reason of men. Mary carried the news to the disciples.

Mary was the herald of the era of grace, of the church, of missions, of world evangelism, of an ascended and glorified Christ, Who has entered upon the throne of His spiritual kingdom. She announced first what has called forth our highest devotion and service ever since.

We have considered Mary as the woman who could not forget. Let us also recall that the Lord's Supper was established by Christ as a symbol of remembrance. He said, "Do this in remembrance of Me, till I come." Just as He is at the center of the Lord's Supper, so He should be at the center of our Christian faith and of our own lives. Mary takes her high place among women and among Christians because she remembered Him at all times, in all places. Can you, then, my friend, forget what He did for you when He died upon the cross and rose from the dead? Can you forget what He is now as Savior, Priest, and King, at the right hand of God? Can you forget what His purposes are in this world in the redemption of man? If you have forgotten, cast yourself at His feet now, and with a touch of faith cling to Christ and worship Him in gratitude and love.

If I forget Gethsemane,
If I forget Thine agony,
If I forget Thy love to me,
Lead me, O Lord, to Calvary.

Yes, and lead me, Lord, to Thy feet in worship.

X

THE NOBLEST WOMAN OF ALL

A sword shall pierce through thine own soul also.

THE title, "The Noblest Woman of All," has always been conceded to Mary, the mother of our Lord. Mary richly deserves her high place of exaltation among women. Mary is called in the Bible, "The mother of our Lord." This does not entitle her to worship nor does it give sanction to all the legends about the person of Mary, but it should cause us to give to her honor and praise and exaltation, which is her due. Because two branches of the Christian church have unduly exalted Mary to the position of deity, we who cling to the Bible teaching are not to go to the other extreme of depreciating Mary. Some of the early fathers, such as Tertullian, Origen, and Chrysostom, did this very thing. Mary deserves an exceedingly high place, and we have no right to deny it to her. Certainly whatever could be attained to or exercised by any woman must have been Mary's status before she was graciously chosen by God to be overshadowed by the Holy Ghost and to become the mother of the Lord Jesus Christ.

For many centuries the Roman Catholic Church believed that Mary's conception was also miraculous, but in 1854 it accepted the dogma of the immaculate conception. This dogma states that Mary's person was not cursed by original sin and that she came into this world different from any other man or woman who bears the responsibility of original guilt and pollution. Mary is given a unique place in the human race. This dogma is based upon the text in Luke, "Blessed art thou among women." It is true that the Bible calls Mary "highly favored," "blessed among women," and designates her as an object of divine grace, but it never puts her in this unique category, that is given to her by Christendom. The main fact that invalidates this teaching is that if it was possible for Mary to be born without sin and to remain sinless throughout her entire life because of a special enduement of the grace of God, then there would have been no necessity for the coming of a Savior. The one and only Person who lived without sin was the Lord Jesus Christ. This same branch of Christendom teaches that Mary was assumed into heaven or taken up into heaven without death. About this the Bible certainly has nothing to say, and the only evidence is that of a late tradition that arose because no one knows where Mary was buried, and because it was a revolting thought to men that the body of Mary, out of which was taken the body of the Lord Jesus Christ, should be subject unto corruption. In itself, we have no objection to either of these doctrines, for they would be perfectly possible with God, but we find no necessity for attempting to re-enforce the character and person of Mary by such hypotheses, which have no basis in the Bible.

There can be no doubt, however, that Mary was a special object of the grace of God. Her choice was an act of election on the part of the Lord. Mary was highly favored because she was the recipient of this divine selection and grace. She was to be closest to the Son of God during His earthly life and was to share His filial affection during His years in the Nazareth home. Mary's reply to the angel, "Be it unto me according to thy word," reveals that she was a woman of faith. She accepted the announcement of God to her concerning this great wonder of a virgin birth and the coming of the Son of God. Hence, when Elisabeth greeted her, she said, "Blessed is she that believed, for there shall be a performance of those things which were told her from the Lord." We acknowledge that Mary's faith was

The Noblest Woman Of All

a gift from almighty God and there was no merit in it, but from the very beginning, Mary believed.

Many were the women who had hoped from the beginning of creation, when Eve received the protoevangelium, that they might be the mother of the Messiah. This was the hope of Sarah; again of Hannah, again of Elisabeth, and of others throughout the centuries, but God looked down o'er the human race and chose the one lone, demure, Jewish maiden from the town of Nazareth, and we ask why. The answer can only be, if we exclude the sovereign grace of God, that God looks upon the heart. In looking upon the heart of Mary, what did He see? The record concerning her suggests to us that He saw first, *A Pure Heart;* second, He saw *A Pondering, Meditative, Heart;* and third, He saw *A Pierced Heart of Sympathetic Suffering.*

I. THE PURE HEART OF THIS NOBLE WOMAN

Sacred art traditionally depicts the angel of the annunciation presenting Mary with a branch of a lily as an emblem of her purity. Well may we consider her as such. Either one of two alternatives must be taken concerning Mary. She is the purest and the highest of women or else Mary must be considered a common harlot. To even suggest the latter is to raise indignation in the heart of a true Christian, and yet that is the suggestion made by every preacher and every teacher who denies the Virgin Birth of our Lord. In the third century A.D., when Origen was refuting the charges brought by a heathen, Celsus, against the Christians, he spoke of the allegation by Celsus that Jesus was born of Mary and a Roman soldier, by name Penthera. This simply means that He was born out of wedlock and was illegitimate. It is a rather crass thing to make such a statement concerning One who has taken such a high place in the minds of millions of people throughout the world, but the same statement is made in a refined way whenever one teaches that Jesus was not born as the Bible says He was born. If the Lord Jesus Christ was not Joseph's son, and if he was born not of the unique, creative power of God, then He was an illegitimate son of Mary. Thus you see that you must either accept the Bible and Christian teaching about the noble life of Mary or you must repudiate both her and the Lord Jesus Christ.

If we accept the purity of Mary, then we have the great Christian doctrine of a Virgin Birth. When it became known to Joseph that Mary was with child, he contemplated putting her away, not publicly, but privately. We may be well assured that there must have been a very heartbreaking scene between these two lowly lovers of Nazareth, Joseph kindly but firmly making an accusation and wrongfully deciding that he could never have Mary as his wife, hurt though this terrible fact did. We may assume that it was on account of this that Mary took her trip to Elisabeth in the hill country of Judah. With what a heavy heart and a fearful soul she must have traversed those hills and vales on the long road leading down through Samaria, past the well of Sychar, through Jerusalem, over the Mount of Olives and on to Bethlehem, and then into the mountains of Judah. Her heart was heavy because of Joseph's action. Her fears were keen because of the shame which would come to her in the world, and yet there was always the reassuring message of the angel that had been given to her and the confidence of her faith that the God Who now was fulfilling His prophecies would care also for her. This gives some conception of what it must have meant to Mary to have these days of fellowship, of communion, and of personal comfort in the presence of her cousin Elisabeth, who also had received a message from the angel, which message confirmed that which was given to Mary, the ever present evidence of which was the dumb Zacharias sitting under his fig tree or going about the house.

The Virgin Birth as taught in the Bible will ever remain a fundamental doctrine of the church. This is not only

The Noblest Woman Of All

because it is a sign but because it is essential to the being of the Savior. Eight centuries before, the prophet had said, "This shall be a sign unto you. A virgin shall conceive and bear a Son, and shall call His name Immanuel." This prophecy to the Davidic house and to women of Israel accounts for the immediate acceptance by Mary of the angelic announcement and also by Joseph of the angel's command. The expectation of a Virgin Birth was in the Hebrew Scriptures. When it actually occurred it was inscripturated as a fact in the narratives of Matthew and of Luke. There is no possible way by which the Virgin Birth may be deleted from these narratives. The Virgin Birth was early accepted by the church, and it has always been accepted. The Apostolic Fathers, the Apologists, and the Fathers of the church all believed in the Virgin Birth, as their own statements testify. It is true that as early as the time of Justin Martyr, namely, 150 A.D., it was spoken against, but the very Simeon said that this Child should be a sign spoken against, and of all the doctrines in the Bible probably this one has been singled out for more ridicule and more opposition than any other. It has been said that it was derived from paganism and that because Jesus was a great personality, men decided that He must have been descended from a god, as Persis or Plato or Alexander were declared to be descended from heathen deities. Men have pointed out the differences in the genealogies, and that both of them claim that Jesus was descended from Joseph rather than Mary. They have argued the impossibility of a Virgin Birth and also have declared that since the rest of the Bible is silent upon this subject, it could not have taken place, but all such arguments overlook the fact that the Virgin Birth was an absolute essential to the Person of Christ as the Son of God. Without this teaching we have a human Jesus, we have a sinful Mary, and we have a fallible Bible. With this doctrine as the basis of our faith, we have a Christ Who is Immanuel, that is, "God with us."

The meaning of the Virgin Birth is that God is with us, that the Incarnation has taken place, and that once in time the eternal Deity became flesh and dwelt among us, that He suffered as we suffer, that He died and rose again. Quite truly we may see that this Child of Mary was God. The whole composite picture proves this—the picture of His miracles, of His sinlessness, of His teaching, of His death upon the cross, and of His resurrection from the dead. He likewise claimed to be God. He claimed to have the authority to speak for God, and He declared that He was equal with the Father. Had Jesus been born of any earthly father, there is no sense in which He could actually have been what He claimed to be and what His life declared Him to be. On the other hand, Jesus was as truly a man as He was God. He received Mary's flesh and blood, and He was subject to temptations and trials and sorrows just as any other man. In fact, He was the perfect representative of all mankind. In Christ thus there were two natures in one Person, the nature of God and the nature of man. Well has this been pointed out by one Bible teacher in reference to the first promise concerning the Messiah. It says in Genesis that the seed of the woman should bruise the head of the serpent. Now it is obvious to all that a woman does not have seed, but is like the earth. She receives the seed, which when planted grows and bears fruit in life. Thus in the very first promise given in the garden of Eden, we have the implication of a Virgin Birth, for it does not say the seed of the man, but the seed of a woman, which would be absurd and a manifest impossibility were it not by the direct, creative power of God. This God-man is Immanuel, or "God with us," the Savior. He is the fleshly representative of true humanity, and He is a real representative of true Deity through the Holy Ghost, such a Being that God could place upon Him the tremendous value which He did in order to bring about the atonement and the satisfaction of Divine law for the human race. Thus we say that the

Incarnation was the only way. Accept the purity of Mary, and you must go on to the great doctrine of the Incarnation. Or, if you accept the doctrine of the coming of God into the world in the form of the human Jesus, then you must accept the doctrine of Mary's purity and of the Virgin Birth.

II. THE PONDERING HEART OF THIS NOBLE WOMAN

If there is any clew to the reason Mary was chosen by God to become the mother of the Lord, it would be contained in the statement, "She pondered all these things in her heart." Such pondering followed the salutation of the angel, the prophecy of Simeon, and the sayings of the boy Jesus. It reveals a meditative, devout, modest, reticent, worshipful, Jewish maiden, who was the example of all that is best in woman. We hold that Mary symbolizes all that is good and pure and beautiful in motherhood.

Perhaps Mary had more about which to ponder in connection with the birth of her Son than other mothers have in connection with the birth of their children, but there is sufficient of the mysterious, the supernatural, and the wonderful in the life of any child to cause a mother's heart to ponder over whence that life came, where it would go, and what it would be while it was here upon earth. How often as we look into the life of a little child being presented for Christian baptism, we wonder what will be the future for that life. Will it be hardship and shame or will it be honor and fame?

Thus it was no doubt that Mary presented her Child in the Temple and looked into the dim future to ascertain the meaning of the angelic annunciation concerning this life. The wondrous light which had appeared unto her and out of which came the angel Gabriel while she had prayed and read her Scriptures, lingered long over her life. In response to her question, "How shall this be?" those words, "The Holy Ghost shall come upon thee, and the power of the

Highest shall overshadow thee: therefore also that holy thing that shall be born of thee shall be called the Son of God . . . for with God nothing is impossible," contained such a depth of meaning that, ponder as she would, Mary could not ascertain the fulness thereof. Who has done more than that today concerning the doctrine of the kenosis or the emptying of Himself and the taking upon Himself of human flesh by Christ? We cannot criticize this Jewish maiden for lack of understanding. Mary must also have pondered in her heart the salutation of Elisabeth when she said, "Blessed art thou among women, and blessed is the fruit of thy womb. And whence is this to me, that the mother of my Lord should come to me?" Here again were words that designated her Child as the Messiah. How Mary must have pondered when the shepherds came to the Bethlehem manger and related that they had seen angels and heard an annunciation, saying, "Glory to God in the highest, and on earth peace, good will among men." Again, when the wise men came presenting their gold and their frankincense and myrrh, saying that they had seen a star in the east which signified, according to their knowledge, that the Christ, the King of the Jews, was born. Then, finally, how she must have pondered as she presented this wonderful Babe in the Temple and heard Simeon say, "Lord, now lettest Thou Thy servant depart in peace, according to Thy Word: for mine eyes have seen Thy salvation, which Thou hast prepared before the face of all people." Again and again throughout Mary's life she pondered and repondered these events which had come to her, that, like the prophets, she might know how the Spirit which was in her did signify that these things should come to pass.

Mary's was a high state of faith, for she believed, due to her meditations upon the Lord Jesus Christ. She believed what the angel said about Him and thus was convinced that this was to be a Virgin Birth and her Son was

The Noblest Woman Of All 143

to be the Son of God. She did not declare this unto others, but kept it in her own heart, quietly meditating upon its meaning. Moreover, Mary believed from the very beginning in the Messiahship of her Son, with all that the Scriptures promised to be fulfilled through Him. She may have wondered why the kingdom was not established, why all the Old Testament prophecies about that kingdom were not fulfilled if her Son were the King, and yet, in spite of it all, she commanded the servants of the house at Cana of Galilee, saying, "Whatsoever He saith unto you, do it." Mary knew that when Jesus undertook to solve a problem, it was always solved. There the lack of wine was fulfilled by His turning the water into wine, an act of omnipotence. Yes, Mary believed in her own Son because she had pondered much upon Him.

One's belief and one's thoughts always lead to one's actions. Thus it was that obedience marked the life of Mary. She obeyed the Holy Spirit in the annunciation by the angel, saying, "Be it unto me according to Thy word." She obeyed the Lord Jesus Christ when He commanded her to now be subject unto John, His beloved disciple. Mary also was very understanding of the Lord Jesus Christ. Even in the days when she did not know what it meant when He said, "Wist ye not that I must be about My Father's business?" she did not seem to question deeper but waited until He should tell her more. She also persevered in her faith. Even during the time of the waning of Jesus' popularity, during His trial, His scourging, and His crucifixion, she remained with Him to the end. When others called Him a malefactor and ridiculed Him, Mary stood at His cross, blessing Him and weeping for Him. Mary was even true to her Son and to His disciples after His death, for she remained with them in the Upper Room, praying for ten days for the coming of the Holy Ghost. She was the recipient along with the apostles of this great blessing. It is true that Mary is not given any prominent place thereafter in the whole of the Scriptures, nor is she even referred to in the Acts or in the Epistles, except at this time at Pentecost, but we may be sure that as Mary's life wore on she did not lose the attribute of pondering over events that had occurred to her earlier.

III. THE PIERCED HEART OF THIS NOBLE WOMAN

Simeon had said to her, when she presented the Lord in the Temple, "A sword shall pierce through thine own soul also." On the cross, we read, "One of the soldiers with a spear pierced His side, and forthwith there came out blood and water." We know that the heart of Christ was truly pierced by a spear. Was Mary's also pierced, and if so, how? Is it not strange that whoever comes near to Jesus Christ has always to drink some cup of sorrow or to have a pierced heart? Think of how Mary's heart was pierced and of how Joseph's soul was pierced by a sword. Each of the disciples was also made to drink the cup of woe, and that cup of suffering exists for believers unto this day.

We may be sure that when Jesus' heart was pierced, Mary's was also, because of her complete identification with Him in life. Hers was the parent-child relationship, that which is blood of my blood, bone of my bone, the closest possible in life. Mary had suffered in the birth of Christ. She had suffered during His life, and she suffered in His death. All that befell Him befell her, and their interests were perfectly identified. Mary so believed in Christ that she was one of His disciples, doing the things He was bidding His followers.

Mary as she stood by the cross of Christ, suffering with Him, is an example of all who are called upon to suffer for Christ's sake in this world. Of such Jesus said, "Blessed are ye, when men shall revile you, and persecute you, and say all manner of evil against you falsely, for my sake." Paul added, "We are the children of God: and if children, then heirs; heirs of God, and joint heirs with Christ; if so

The Noblest Woman Of All

be that we suffer with him that we may be glorified together." Again Paul said, "I fill up that which is behind of the afflictions of Christ in my flesh for his body's sake which is the church." There is a very real sense in which that must be done by us all. This suffering is not one of pity, it is a lifting of the world's load of sin and trouble. In Christ we are unified one with another in the bearing of one another's burdens for Christ's sake. If we are thoroughly identified with our Lord we will suffer with Him here. Unquestionably this is the meaning of taking up our Cross and of being baptized with the baptism that He was baptized with.

It is true that Christ suffered directly in the stead of many, and of us. He died outside the gate that he might sanctify the people with His own blood. Sin pierced his heart, and by the shedding of that blood, he made an atonement for our sins. Atonement in the Bible is always by the blood which represents the life of man poured out in satisfaction for guilt, and it is atonement alone that reconciles the sinner to God. The sufferings of Christ were substitutionary. He was the lonely sufferer, the one suffering for the many. It was a sufficient atonement. It was efficacious and He will save those for whom he died. Though our sufferings are qualitatively different, nevertheless, we are exhorted to "go forth unto him without the camp, bearing his reproach." In a real sense we are to bear His reproach and His sufferings although these are not atoning sufferings. To be so stirred that we will take that position is a gift from God. We know that His sufferings were for us and therefore we are willing to bear His reproach. The closer we come to following the example of Jesus, to attaining to a sense of social solidarity, to identifying ourselves with the sins and shortcomings of men, the more we will be persecuted and the more we will suffer for it. I repeat that this is not for the sake of atonement, but it is for the sake of morally expressing the Cross in our lives.

On the cross, we behold also a Christ Who is sympathetically suffering for His own mother. There He succored her as well as substituted for her. If the Captain of our salvation was made perfect through suffering, suffering must be a part of life. We conceive of life as a trial. Man is born to trouble as the sparks fly upward. Suffering must add something to life and character, here and hereafter, and it is only the cross of Christ that gives the explanation of all this vicarious suffering in the world. Like as Christ succored His own mother from the cross, so all who will turn to Him can be succored in the time of their suffering and their need. With this perfect knowledge and sympathy for what we pass through, He can provide for our need. Thus His invitation is given to us to come boldly to the throne of grace and to ask for mercy and grace to help in time of need. It is true that Jesus empowers us to endure a pierced heart. No suffering for the believer can be too much, for all suffering is transformed into glory. Thus we endure these light afflictions, which are for the moment, because they work out a far more exceeding and eternal weight of glory. Mary's experience of a pierced heart tells us that she was compelled to suffer along with her Son and with others who are in need but that she was able to endure that affliction of heart in triumph because of the grace given to her by Christ, her Son and Lord.

Here, then, we see the noblest woman of all, the woman whose life fulfilled all that God promised to the women of the Old Testament who were good and precious and noble and true. Her Son was her own Savior and Lord, just as He may be yours and He may be mine.

www.ingramcontent.com/pod-product-compliance
Lightning Source LLC
Chambersburg PA
CBHW050828160426
43192CB00010B/1936